Australia's WILD WEIRD WONDERFUL WEATHER

For Erryn and his boys, Kai and Louie,
who always have an eye on the weather
—SOR

For Riley and his sense of weather wonder
—TM

Our gratitude goes to our country's children,
who hold the future of our climate in their hands.

Australia's WILD WEIRD WONDERFUL WEATHER

Stephanie Owen Reeder
+
Tania McCartney

NLA PUBLISHING

Whatever the Weather

Whether the weather be fine
Or whether the weather be not,
Whether the weather be cold
Or whether the weather be hot,
We'll weather the weather
Whatever the weather,
Whether we like it or not!

ANONYMOUS

Contents

SEASONAL WEATHER
- 8 Whatever Is Weather?
- 10 Bush Forecasting
- 12 Feeling Hot, Hot, Hot!

PRECIPITATION
- 16 Under a Cloud
- 18 Singing in the Rain
- 20 Shiver Me Timbers!

SOUND, LIGHT, MOVEMENT
- 24 Lighting Up the Sky
- 26 Nature's Fireworks
- 28 Blow, Wind, Blow!

DISASTROUS WEATHER
- 32 Rogue Weather
- 34 Extreme Australia
- 36 Weatherproofing

WEATHER FORECASTING
- 40 Animal Antics
- 42 Measuring Up
- 44 Reading the Weather

CLIMATE CHANGE
- 48 A Warming World
- 50 Learning from Nature
- 52 Weathering the Future

RESEARCHING WEATHER
- 56 Exploring the Weather
- 60 Weather Words
- 62 Weather Resources

- 64 Index

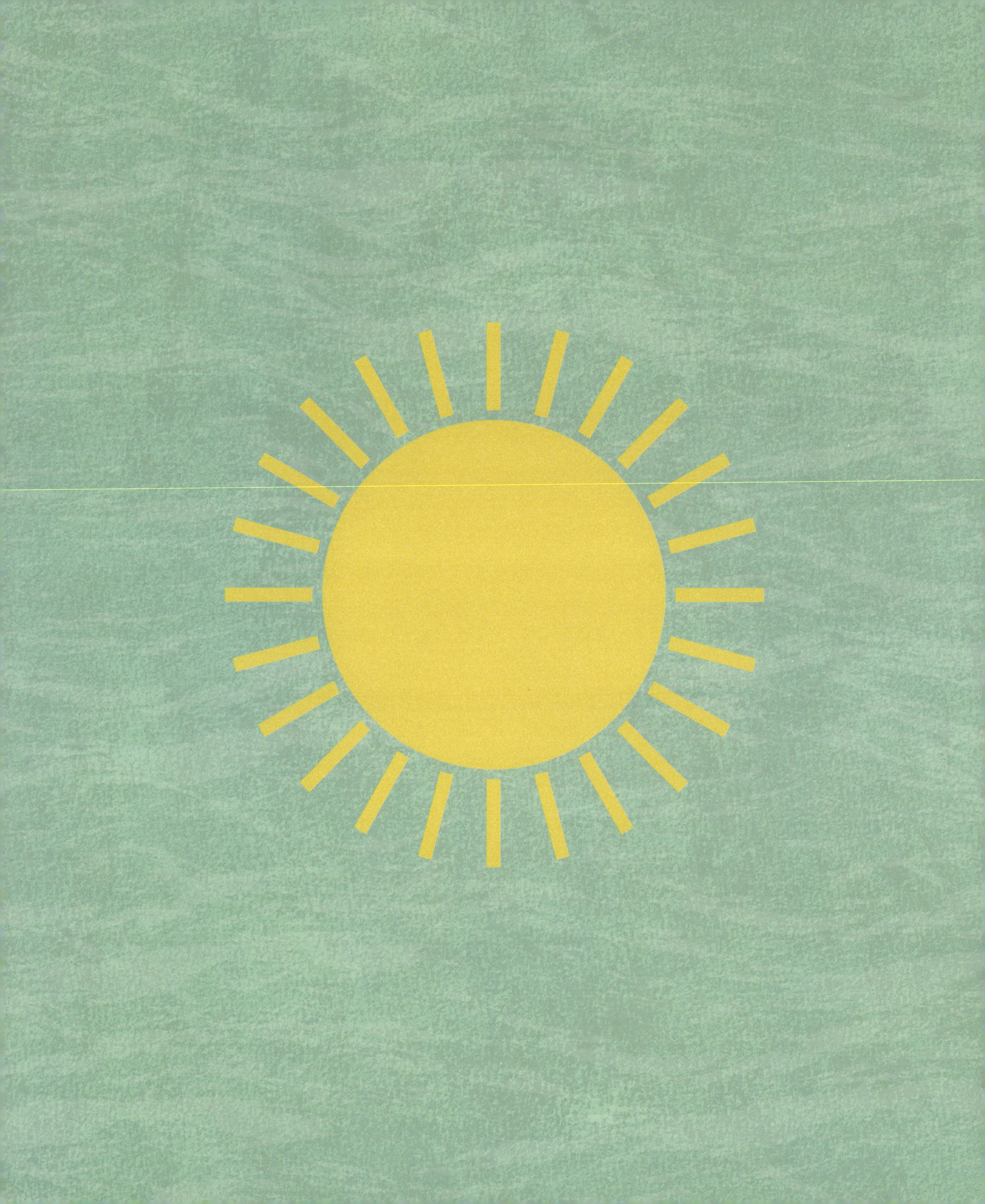

Seasonal Weather

It never seems to rain in reason. We get droughts one year and floods next season.

THE GNOWANGERUP STAR AND TAMBELLUP-ONGERUP GAZETTE, 1940

Whatever Is Weather?

WEATHER affects us every day in every way. It dictates what we wear, what we eat, where we play and even how we feel. It's in the air all around us—the **ATMOSPHERE**. Whether it's hot or cold, wet or fine, windy or still, there is no escaping the weather!

ATMOSPHERICS

- 78% NITROGEN
- 21% OXYGEN
- 1% NEON, ARGON, HELIUM, KRYPTON, METHANE, HYDROGEN, CARBON DIOXIDE

The atmosphere is made up of **GASES**. The correct balance of these gases is essential for life on Earth.

TOUCHED BY THE SUN

Even though it's **150 MILLION KILOMETRES** away, the **SUN**'s energy fuels weather here on Earth. The sun's **RADIATION** provides heat and light, and powers winds and storms.

THE SILLY SEASONS

Early European settlers in Australia transplanted the four seasons they were familiar with: **SPRING, SUMMER, AUTUMN** and **WINTER**. However, these seasons only apply to temperate climatic zones in southern Australia. In the Top End, non-Indigenous Australians identify two seasons, **WET** and **DRY**, while Indigenous people—like the Bininj/Mungguy of Kakadu—identify SIX or more.

KAKADU'S SIX SEASONS

1. **GUDJEWG** MONSOONAL
2. **BANGGERRENG** STORMY
3. **YEGGE** COOL
4. **WURRGENG** COLD
5. **GURRUNG** HOT AND DRY
6. **GUNUMELENG** HOT AND HUMID

TWO SEASONS
1. 2.

FOUR SEASONS
1. 2. 3. 4.

SIX SEASONS
1. 2. 3. 4. 5. 6.

SWIRLING CLOUDS

Because the Earth is tilted on its axis, the hottest parts are closest to the **EQUATOR**. Driven by the sun's heat, the Earth's atmosphere carries hot air from the equator towards the **POLES** and cold air from the poles to the equator. This can be seen from **SPACE** as swirling masses of clouds.

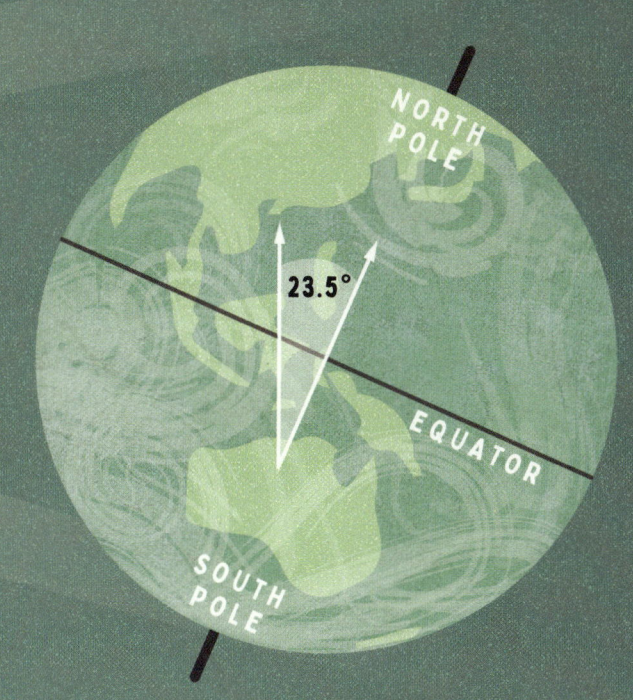

NORTH POLE
23.5°
EQUATOR
SOUTH POLE

THERMOSPHERE

MESOSPHERE

STRATOSPHERE
OZONE LAYER

TROPOSPHERE

SPHERES OF INFLUENCE

Weather hangs out in the **TROPOSPHERE**—the part of the atmosphere closest to Earth. Above it is the **STRATOSPHERE**, with its thin blanket of ozone that protects us from the sun's more harmful rays. Above them are the **MESOSPHERE**, which helps stop meteors plummeting to Earth, and the **THERMOSPHERE**.

- EQUATORIAL
- TROPICAL
- SUBTROPICAL
- DESERT
- GRASSLAND
- TEMPERATE

CLIMATIC CONDITIONS

We experience weather every day, but **CLIMATE** is based on average weather conditions over many years. According to the Bureau of Meteorology, Australia has **SIX CLIMATIC ZONES**.

When you hold out your hand, you're supporting 1,000 kilograms of **AIR PRESSURE**. Luckily, the pressure inside your body equals the pressure outside it, so you don't get squashed flat!

1,000KG

Bush Forecasting

INDIGENOUS AUSTRALIANS have inhabited this continent for over 60,000 years. During that time, they've adapted to living on the **DRIEST INHABITED CONTINENT** in the world. They've farmed, conserved, managed and learnt from the land while honouring Country.

CELEBRATING THE SEASONS

Indigenous people developed **SEASONAL CALENDARS** specific to the areas they lived in and the life cycles of the plants and animals that flourished there. For example, there are **SIX SEASONS** in the Gariwerd calendar.

BALLAMBAR — BUTTERFLY SEASON — EARLY SUMMER — NOVEMBER – JANUARY

PETYAN — WILDFLOWER SEASON — SPRING — SEPTEMBER – NOVEMBER

LARNEUK — NESTING BIRD SEASON — PRE-SPRING — JULY – AUGUST

DANCING IN THE DESERT

Many European explorers died of thirst in the **DESERT** while searching for the elusive 'Inland Sea'. However, Indigenous people living in Central Australia knew how to locate water in even the harshest conditions. When these water sources dried up, they turned to the **RAINMAKERS**—dancers who they believed could conjure up storm clouds from a clear sky. In some parts of Australia, this **TRADITIONAL KNOWLEDGE** is still passed on.

GARIWERD SEASONS, THE GRAMPIANS, VICTORIA

KOOYANG
frogs croak, kangaroos box, swamp lilies flower, beetles emerge, eels abound

GWANGAL MORONN
berries ripen, fungi pop up, tortoises hibernate, tadpoles wriggle, birds moult

CHUNNUP
waters rise, rain falls, mists drift in, sugar gliders breed, magpies swoop

LARNEUK
rivers run high, orchids flower, caterpillars emerge, ducklings paddle

PETYAN
trees flower, bees swarm, platypuses lay eggs, baby koalas leave pouches

BALLAMBAR
butterflies abound, reptiles sunbathe, seed pods open, midges swarm

WISDOM OF THE ELDERS

The **BUREAU OF METEOROLOGY** has complex instruments and computer models for measuring and forecasting weather. It also studies **INDIGENOUS WEATHER KNOWLEDGE** to learn about changes in the climate caused by both natural phenomena and human activity.

ANIMAL BAROMETERS

Some Indigenous people predict seasonal changes by observing **ANIMAL BEHAVIOUR**. In western Arnhem Land, the arrival of **ALYURR**—brightly coloured grasshoppers—marks the coming of the wet season. In the Grampians, the rainy season is heralded by **BLACK COCKATOOS**, their blood-red tail feathers flashing as they descend upon the flowering wattle trees.

The gidgee, or **WATTLE TREE**, reacts to a rise in humidity by 'sweating' a sharp-smelling sap—a sign that rain is coming

KOOYANG
EEL SEASON
LATE SUMMER
JANUARY – MARCH

GWANGAL MORONN
HONEY BEE SEASON
AUTUMN
MARCH – MAY

CHUNUUP
COCKATOO SEASON
WINTER
MAY – JULY

ELEMENTAL CREATURES

Indigenous weather knowledge is handed down through art, dance, song, ceremony and stories. The **DREAMING STORIES** of Arnhem Land feature powerful ancestral beings such as **GOORIALLA**, the Rainbow Serpent, who creates rain clouds, and **NAMARRGON**, the Lightning Man, who uses stone axes to make thunder and lightning.

FLOOD FORECASTING

Thousands of years of experience taught the **WIRADJURI PEOPLE** of southern New South Wales to respect the flood-prone Murrumbidgee River. They tried to pass on their knowledge to European settlers, but were ignored. In June 1852, a torrent of water swallowed the town of **GUNDAGAI**. Four Wiradjuri men in bark canoes risked their lives to pluck stranded people from trees and rooftops. After the **FLOOD**, the settlers rebuilt on higher ground.

Feeling Hot, Hot, Hot!

While around 70 per cent of **AUSTRALIA** is arid or semi-arid, with very little rainfall, weather across the continent can vary significantly in **SUMMER**. We can have stifling humidity in the tropics, heatwaves in Central Australia, balmy beach days on the coast and dustings of snow on the mountains.

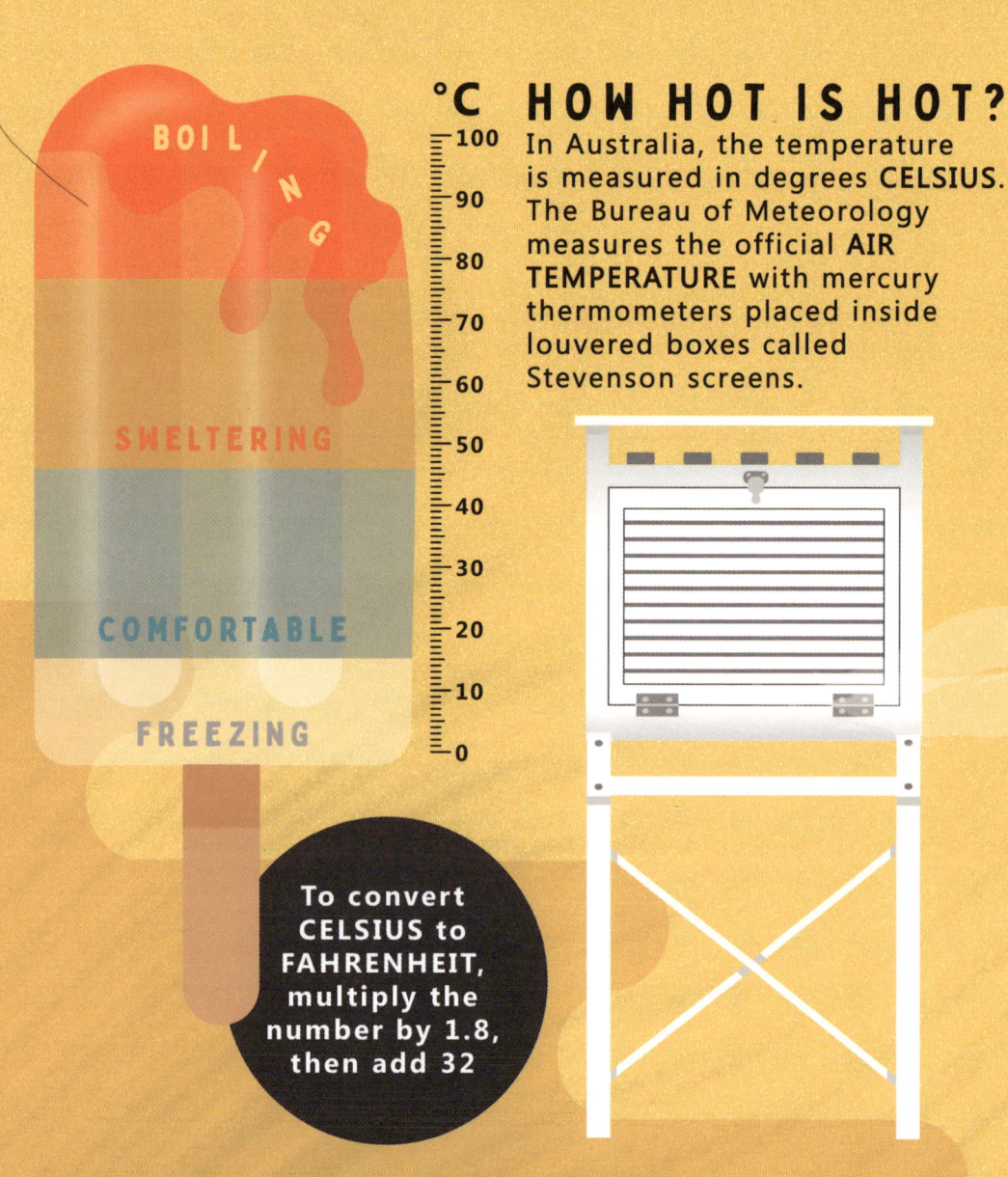

BOILING
SWELTERING
COMFORTABLE
FREEZING

HOW HOT IS HOT?
In Australia, the temperature is measured in degrees **CELSIUS**. The Bureau of Meteorology measures the official **AIR TEMPERATURE** with mercury thermometers placed inside louvered boxes called Stevenson screens.

To convert **CELSIUS** to **FAHRENHEIT**, multiply the number by 1.8, then add 32.

HOW HOT DOES IT FEEL?
TEMPERATURE is measured in two ways. The 'actual', or **AMBIENT**, temperature is measured with a thermometer kept in the shade. The 'feels like', or **APPARENT**, temperature is based on how hot or cold the air actually feels when **WIND CHILL** and **HUMIDITY** are taken into account.

FIRE DANGER RATING
- LOW-MODERATE: 0–11
- HIGH: 12–24
- VERY HIGH: 25–49
- SEVERE: 50–74
- EXTREME: 75–99
- CATASTROPHIC: 100+

BLAZING BUSHFIRES
BUSHFIRES thrive when the temperature is high, humidity low and strong winds blow. Tinder-dry native bushes and flammable eucalyptus trees add to the mix. In summer, **OUT-OF-CONTROL** bushfires can threaten people, buildings, animals and the environment. During the 2019/2020 **BUSHFIRE SEASON**, over 200 ferocious fires caused death and destruction across Australia.

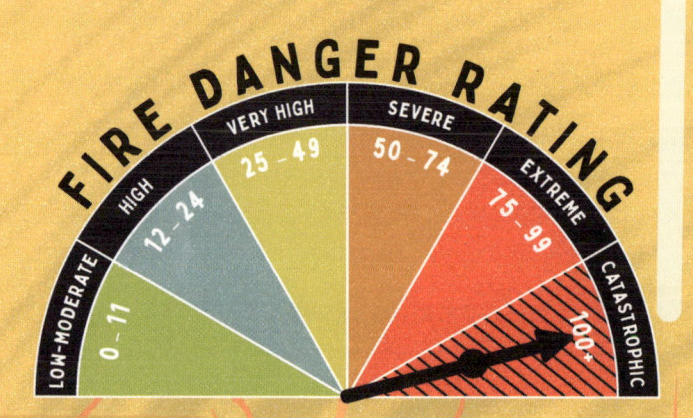

STICKY TROPICS

The human body sweats to cool down, so dry heat is often easier to cope with than humid heat. In high **HUMIDITY**, sweat doesn't evaporate effectively, so it's easy to overheat. This is a particular problem in **TROPICAL REGIONS** during the wet season.

HARMFUL HEAT

A **HEATWAVE** is three or more days with unusually high maximum and minimum temperatures. The **BUREAU OF METEOROLOGY**'s heatwave service runs from November to March. It shows where the heatwaves are and gives advice on how to **SURVIVE** them.

DESERT DIVAS

There are ten **DESERTS** in **CENTRAL AUSTRALIA**. The largest, the Great Victoria Desert, stretches across Western Australia into South Australia. Australian deserts are home to well-adapted native animals and over a million **FERAL CAMELS**, which thrive in the harsh conditions.

GREAT VICTORIA DESERT

During a **HEATWAVE** in Cairns in November 2018, around 23,000 **SPECTACLED FLYING FOXES** suffered from heatstroke and fell out of their trees, **DEAD**

DAMAGING DROUGHTS

Parts of Australia regularly experience **DROUGHTS** that last for years. As **WATER LEVELS** drop in rivers, fish and other freshwater creatures die. Crops fail, dams dry up, and sheep and cattle have to be handfed. Native animals also run out of food and water, trees wither and die, and soil is **ERODED**.

Precipitation

It is reported that the hail completely stripped a large standing crop of wheat, whilst all fruit in the storm area was knocked off the trees. Young turkeys and chickens were killed in large numbers, and in places potatoes were washed out of the ground.

THE YASS COURIER, 1910

Under a Cloud

CLOUDS are made of thousands of tiny droplets of moisture mixed with dust, dirt, pollen and plant fragments. They come in all shapes and sizes—from cottonballs and cauliflowers to sheets and blankets. The five main types of cloud have LATIN NAMES.

CIRRUS clouds are feathery WISPS of white.

STRATUS clouds layer the sky in SHEETS.

NIMBUS clouds are the dark bringers of RAIN.

ALTO clouds join with other clouds to hover HIGHER.

CUMULUS clouds form in fat FLUFFY piles.

Cloud cover called anti-cyclonic gloom makes MELBOURNE Australia's most OVERCAST city

COW CLOUDS
Bubbles of cloud hanging underneath large cloud formations are called MAMMATUS, from the Latin word for udder. They do not rain milk!

BLANKETING THE SKY
When NIMBUS and STRATUS clouds get together, we're in for a dull, grey day. NIMBOSTRATUS clouds cover the sky in a dark blanket that blocks out the sun and brings steady rain.

ANATOMY OF A CLOUD

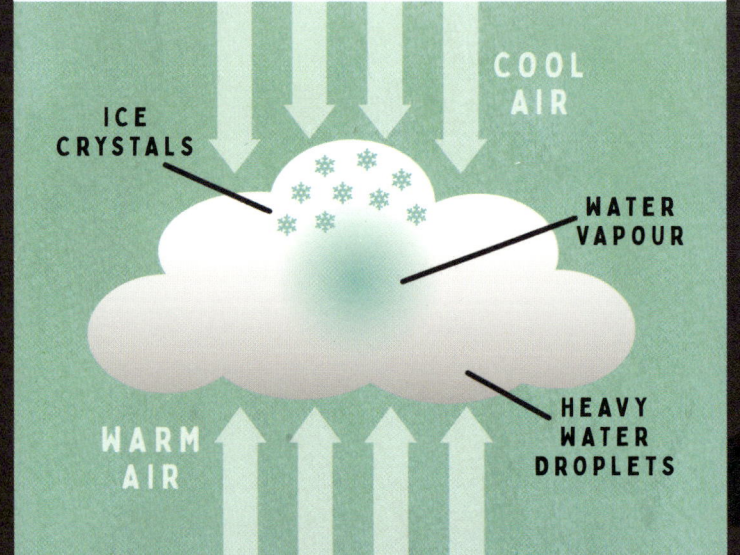

- ICE CRYSTALS
- COOL AIR
- WATER VAPOUR
- WARM AIR
- HEAVY WATER DROPLETS

MARES' TAILS

The Latin word **CIRRUS** means a lock of curly hair. Cirrus clouds sometimes also look like horses' tails, so they're called **CIRRUS UNCINUS**. While these clouds don't produce rain, they're said to herald a storm.

CLOUD CASTLES

As their name implies, **CASTELLANUS** clouds look a little like castles. A combination of all **FIVE** cloud types, they grow vertically, tower upon tower, reaching high into the sky.

LAZY CLOUDS

FOG hangs around near the ground, keeping the air moist and chilly. It makes ordinary things look distorted. It can also be dangerous, swallowing ships at sea and shutting down airports. Fog is a cloud with no altitude but plenty of **ATTITUDE**!

CIRRUS — 13KM

CUMULONIMBUS

CIRROSTRATUS — 10KM

CIRROCUMULUS — 7KM

NIMBOSTRATUS

ALTOSTRATUS — 5KM

ALTOCUMULUS

STRATOCUMULUS — 2KM
STRATUS
CUMULUS
MIST
FOG + SMOG

PILLOW CLOUDS

CUMULUS clouds look like cottonballs or big soft pillows. They're formed by warm air bubbling up until it reaches cold air. The water vapour in the air condenses and makes a **FLUFFY** white cloud.

FISHY SKIES

CIRRUS clouds can form into **VERTEBRATUS** clouds, which look like the skeleton of a fish. And bands of small white fleecy clouds often form patterns like fish scales. Sailors call this a 'mackerel' sky and believe that a **STORM** is brewing.

SMOTHERING SMOG

When **FOG** and **POLLUTION** team up, we get **SMOG**. Smoke, dust, car exhaust and industrial pollutants combine with fog to blanket cities in a choking cloud that can only be removed by a strong wind. Around 3,000 Australians die each year from the effects of this **TOXIC CLOUD!**

THUNDERCLOUDS

When **CUMULUS** team up with **NIMBUS** to form **CUMULONIMBUS** clouds, they get higher and higher, taller and taller, darker and **DARKER**. Raindrops form in the bottom of these clouds and ice crystals in the top. They are the rain bringers, the thunder makers, the lightning strikers.

CLOUD FARMING

During droughts, **CLOUD SEEDING** is sometimes employed to try to make it rain. A plane sprays a likely looking bank of clouds with tiny amounts of chemicals such as silver iodide. This encourages small ice crystals inside the clouds to create life-giving **RAIN**.

Singing in the Rain

Heated by the SUN, water in lakes, streams, rivers, seas and oceans EVAPORATES and is absorbed by the atmosphere as WATER VAPOUR. It then condenses into water droplets inside clouds before falling back to earth. This PRECIPITATION can be rain, sleet, hail or snow.

THE WATER CYCLE

- WATER ON EARTH EVAPORATES
- IT THEN CONDENSES AND FORMS CLOUDS
- WATER FALLS AS RAIN, SLEET AND SNOW
- THIS PRECIPITATION FILLS RIVERS AND SEAS

TASTY RAINDROPS

Artists often draw RAINDROPS shaped like teardrops. In reality, small raindrops are SPHERICAL while they tumble through the sky. As they grow bigger, air pressure flattens their bottoms, so larger raindrops are actually shaped like a HAMBURGER BUN.

DEWY DIAMONDS

DEWDROPS form at night on surfaces close to the ground, where the air is coldest. In deserts, dew provides much-needed water for plants and animals. It also contributes to the weathering of rock formations, as it dribbles down into crevices and FREEZES during the night.

> Check out your SHADOW in the early morning light. DEW on the grass can produce a sparkling HALO of white light around your head

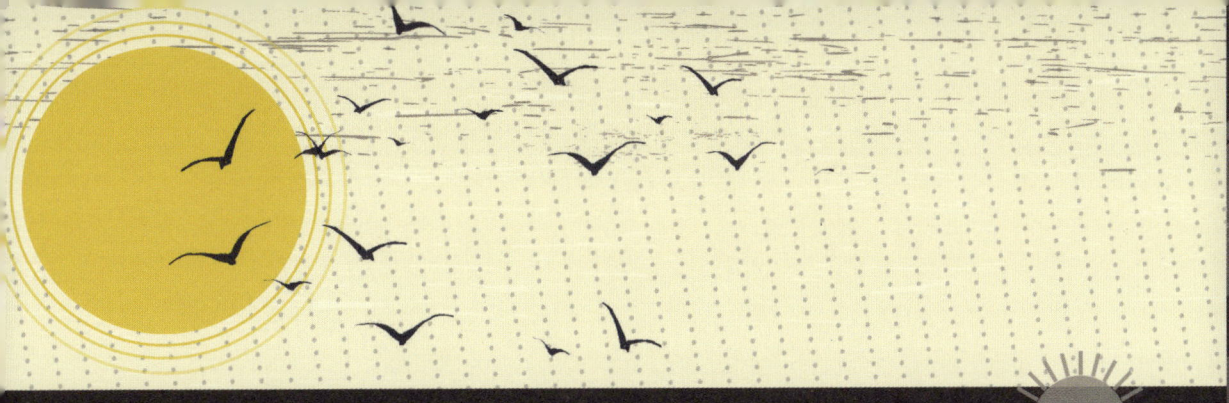

WHERE ARE THE CLOUDS?

Sometimes a light drizzle of rain falls from a cloudless sky. This is called **SEREIN**—a **SUNSHOWER**. The water comes from either an evaporating cloud or moisture being blown from somewhere over the horizon.

RAINING FISH AND FROGS

During a downpour, people often say 'IT'S RAINING CATS AND DOGS'. Pets don't usually drop from the sky, but other **ANIMALS** do. A large **WATERSPOUT** can pick up small creatures like frogs and fish from waterways and deposit them many kilometres away.

SMELLY RAIN

Air pressure drops before it rains. This makes rotten **SMELLS** from ponds, drains and dogs' droppings even more disgusting! To make matters worse, approaching rain causes **HIGHER HUMIDITY**, which makes your sense of smell work better. So if there's a nasty pong in the air, rain may be on its way.

TOO MUCH PRECIPITATION

Storm surges cause **FLOODS** when waves inundate the land, while snow melting in the mountains can flood nearby rivers. Thunderstorms can cause **FLASH FLOODING**, as heavy rain falls on a small area in a very short time. And days and days of steady rain can lead to watercourses overflowing.

DISAPPEARING RAIN

VIRGA is rain that doesn't make it to the ground. The raindrops pass through a dry, warm layer of air and **EVAPORATE** before they land on the thirsty soil below.

In 1964, two Australian scientists invented the word PETRICHOR to describe the scent of rain on hot earth

Shiver Me Timbers!

When temperatures drop in the WINTER months, chilly weather produces icy PHENOMENA such as frost, hail, sleet and snow in southern parts of Australia.

BLINDING SNOW

SNOWFIELDS can be dangerous. Overexposure can lead to HYPOTHERMIA, when the body gets so cold it begins to shut down, or to FROSTBITE, when exposed skin freezes. On a sunny winter's day, you can get both SUNBURN and temporary SNOW BLINDNESS from sunlight reflecting off dazzling white snow.

The tip of an icicle is hollow!

FROZEN DEW

On cold, clear nights, the temperature DROPS and moisture in the air freezes. Surfaces are coated in a sparkling layer of frozen dew called FROST. Although it makes for a chilly start, a frosty morning usually means a fine sunny day.

ICE GARDEN ON A WINDOW

ICY FERN FRONDS

On very cold mornings in alpine areas, feathery ICE GARDENS form on the outside of windows. House eaves and tree branches are festooned with decorative HOARFROST and shards of frozen ICICLES.

GREAT BALLS OF HAIL

Turbulent air currents toss ICE CRYSTALS around inside thunderclouds until they grow so heavy they fall to the ground as HAIL. It can be as small as a PEA or as big as an ORANGE. Because it forms in large thunderclouds, hail can strike at any time of the year.

In June 1836, enough SNOW fell in coastal SYDNEY for children to make snowmen and have snowball fights

The CRYSTALS in snow and ice reflect all the colours of the spectrum equally, so to our eyes they look WHITE

FABULOUS FLAKES

SNOW forms when ice crystals in a cloud collide with each other again and again. They BOND together and, when they're big enough, flutter to the ground as snow. If the air near the ground is too warm, the snow starts melting and falls as SLEET.

SNOWFLAKES come in a vast array of hexagonal shapes, and no two snowflakes are ALIKE

DEADLY BLIZZARDS

BLIZZARDS form when strong winds blow, temperatures are low and there's lots of snow. It's easy to get lost in a blizzard, as the horizon disappears in WHITEOUT conditions. You can also suffocate when dry snow is blown about. And the WIND CHILL FACTOR makes the air feel many degrees colder than it is.

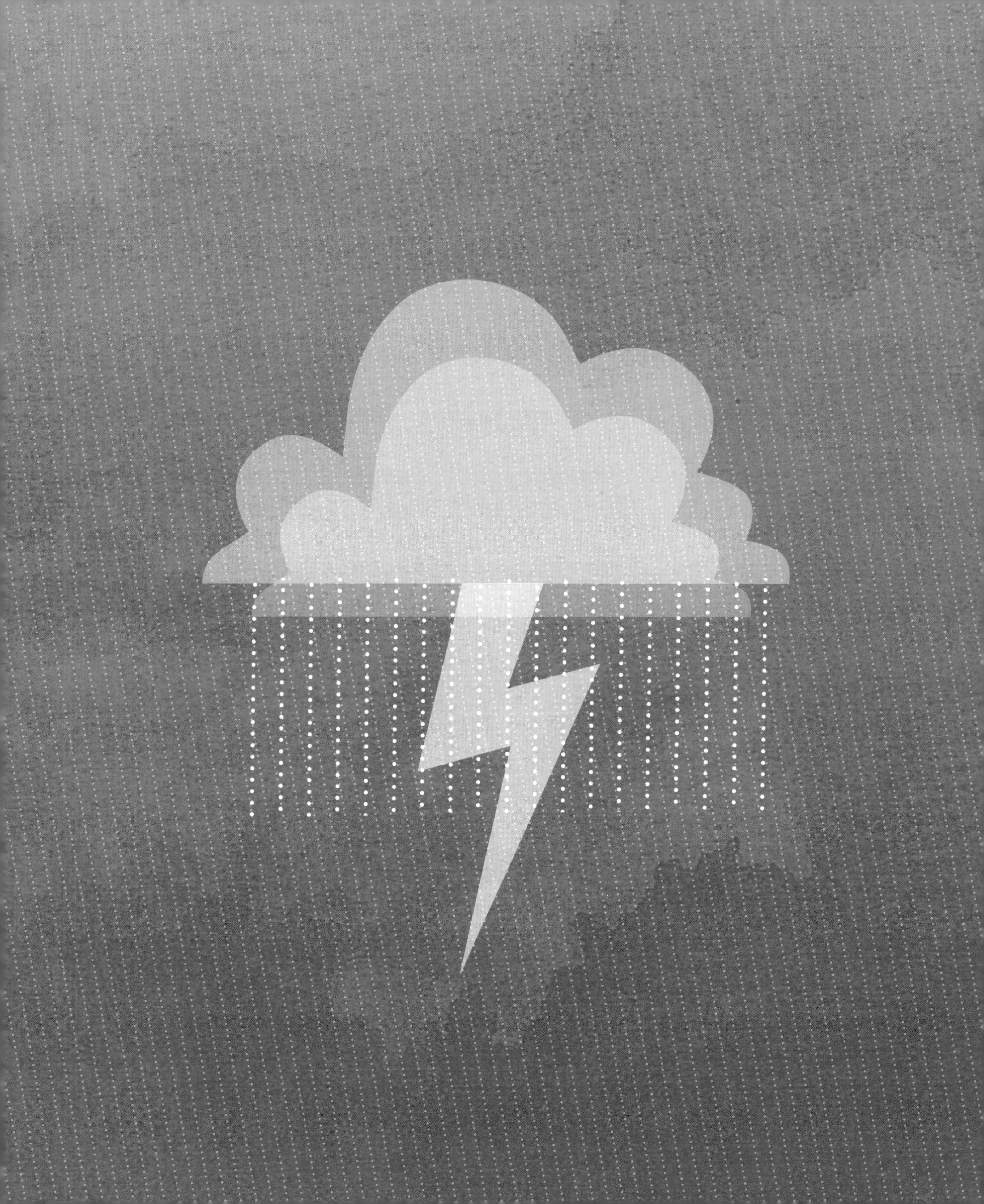

Sound, Light, Movement

The ... ball lightning ... was six feet above the ground, about the size of a watermelon, round, glowed like fire, and then exploded with a blast that sent sparks flying above the heads of several children.

THE DAILY MERCURY (MACKAY), 1953

Lighting Up the Sky

From brilliant blues to dull greys, from stunning reds to gleaming golds, the sky is an ever-changing canvas of COLOUR and LIGHT.

COLOUR PRISMS

RAINDROPS act like tiny glass prisms, breaking up sunlight into the seven colours of the SPECTRUM. The colours bend, with each one reflecting at a different angle. This creates the bands of colour in a RAINBOW.

Like all moths, BOGONGS are attracted to light. Scientists say it may be related to navigation

SOMEWHERE OVER A RAINBOW

The RAINBOW you see depends on the wind, the position of the sun, and where you are standing. This means no two people ever see precisely the SAME rainbow at the same time—we each have our very own.

RED ORANGE YELLOW GREEN BLUE INDIGO VIOLET

ROUND RAINBOWS

A rainbow is actually CIRCULAR, but we can only see half of it as the rest is hiding below the horizon. So, unfortunately, it's impossible to find the end of a rainbow and its legendary pot of GOLD!

CURTAINS OF COLOUR

One of the most amazing things in the night sky is an AURORA—shifting curtains of luminous colours. They usually appear near the two magnetic poles. In the Southern Hemisphere it is called AURORA AUSTRALIS. Auroras form when zippy electrons from the sun collide with gases in the Earth's upper atmosphere.

MOODY MOONBOWS

While sunlight reflecting off raindrops creates rainbows, eerie white arcs of light appear when water droplets reflect the light of the moon or sunlight penetrates a fog. Pale MOONBOWS and FOGBOWS are rarer than their more colourful cousins.

AZURE SKIES

The COLOUR of the sky is caused by sunlight interacting with water vapour and dust particles in the atmosphere. 'White' rays of light break up into the COLOURS of the SPECTRUM. Different colours travel at different WAVELENGTHS—from the longest (red and orange) to the shortest (indigo and violet). Shorter wavelengths scatter more easily across the sky, which is why it usually looks BLUE.

WAVELENGTHS are measured in NANOMETRES, with the wavelength shorter for cool colours and longer for warm colours

SUNRAYS → WATER VAPOUR → DUST → COLOUR SPECTRUM → WAVELENGTHS → BLUE!

400
425
470
550
600
630
665

FIRE IN THE SKY

At SUNRISE and SUNSET, the sun is at a low angle, so its rays have to travel further through the atmosphere. This means that we see more colours at the RED end of the spectrum: yellow, orange and red. Pollution, ash from volcanoes and smoke from bushfires make these colours appear even BRIGHTER.

SUNSET SHOWOFFS

When the SUN is setting, its RAYS appear to FAN out across the horizon. This is an OPTICAL ILLUSION. The rays are actually coming straight down, but they are SCATTERED by water droplets and dust particles in the air.

Nature's Fireworks

LIGHTNING forms when ice crystals jostling around inside towering storm clouds create giant sparks of ELECTRICITY. Lightning can be dangerous, but it also gave us fire for cooking and keeping warm. It might even have created life on Earth!

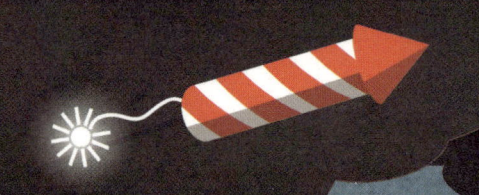

SPARKLING SHEETS
SHEET LIGHTNING is the most common type of lightning. It occurs inside a cloud or between adjacent clouds, and it lights up the sky with an eerie FLICKERING light.

BOUNCING BALLS OF FIRE
BALL LIGHTNING is rare. It floats in the air or rolls along the ground, climbing over objects and 'CHASING' people. Beware—sometimes it explodes!

KA-BOOM!

NOISY SHOCKWAVES
Lightning HEATS the air around it at supersonic speed—to a massive 30,000 degrees Celsius. This makes the air expand until it explodes, causing a booming SHOCKWAVE that we hear as THUNDER. When a storm is far away, you can hear the shockwaves bouncing off the clouds and the ground.

On Christmas Day 2018, DARWIN was hit by a blistering 91,000 lightning strikes

UNZIPPING THE SKY
FORKED LIGHTNING zigzags from cloud to ground. It is less common but more spectacular than sheet lightning. It's sometimes answered by a lightning bolt that goes UP from the ground so fast that you can't see it.

TRACKING THUNDERSTORMS

THUNDER and LIGHTNING occur at the same time. Because light travels faster than sound, we usually see the lightning and THEN hear the thunder. If you can count a three-second gap between a lightning strike and a thunderclap, the storm is about a kilometre away—and it's time to SEEK SHELTER!

TARGET PRACTICE

Lightning likes WARM AIR, so it sometimes comes down chimneys. It's also attracted to other TALL objects that stand out in the landscape, like trees, buildings and aerials—and even umbrellas and golf sticks.

EXPLODING TREES

It's dangerous to stand UNDER A TREE during a THUNDERSTORM. If the tree trunk is hit by a lightning bolt, the sap inside it will heat up, vaporise and EXPLODE.

OFF WITH YOUR SOCKS

A direct LIGHTNING STRIKE can literally blow off your socks—along with the rest of your clothes! Lightning strikes cause around five deaths and 100 INJURIES in Australia each year.

LIGHTNING STRIKES
- IN-CLOUD
- CLOUD-TO-AIR
- CLOUD-TO-CLOUD
- CLOUD-TO-GROUND

AVOIDING THE SIZZLE

If you're OUTSIDE in a thunderstorm, find shelter as quickly as possible. If there's nowhere safe to go, make yourself as small a target as possible by crouching down near the ground. If you're INSIDE, stay away from metal objects and appliances, as lightning can travel down electrical wires.

Blow, Wind, Blow!

WIND is moving air. You can't SEE the wind, but you can see its effects—leaves tossing on a tree or a boat with billowing sails. You can also FEEL the wind—a gentle touch on your cheek or hair whipping across your face. And you can definitely HEAR the wind—a whistle down the chimney or a shrieking wail.

WHAT IS WIND?

Wind is SWIRLING AIR caused by the Earth's surface heating unevenly. As heat is released from the ground, cooler air sinks and warmer air rises. These air masses move from areas of HIGH PRESSURE to areas of LOW PRESSURE, creating everything from breezes and blizzards to gusts and gales.

Boats and planes measure wind in KNOTS. One knot equals 1.85 kilometres per hour, so a 100-knot wind travels at 185 kilometres per hour!

WICKED WHIRLWINDS

Willy-willies, dust devils, waterspouts, twisters, tornadoes, typhoons, cyclones and hurricanes are all WHIRLWINDS. These rotating masses of air move across land or water, picking up whatever's in their way and dumping it somewhere else. A large whirlwind can lift heavy OBJECTS like horses, cars and even houses!

SAND SCULPTURES

Wind squalls in deserts cause SANDSTORMS. Over hundreds of millions of years these storms have helped sculpt monoliths like ULURU and KATA TJUTA in the Northern Territory.

KICKING UP DUST

DUST STORMS happen when hot, dry winds hit a cold front and strip the soil from drought-stricken plains. A great wall of dust rises into the sky, blocking out the sun and covering everything in a choking blanket of DIRT.

In 2009, a massive DUST STORM in eastern Australia blew red dust and soil all the way to New Zealand, where it turned the glaciers pink!

CYCLONIC WINDS

In a **CYCLONE**, air moves around a centre of low pressure, turning clockwise in the Southern Hemisphere and anticlockwise in the Northern Hemisphere. These **SUPERSTORMS** 'breed' in the warm waters of tropical oceans. With wind gusts of up to 300 kilometres per hour, cyclones are destructive powerhouses.

CHILLY WINDS

When strong winds blow on a cold day, **WIND CHILL** makes the **APPARENT TEMPERATURE** plummet. So if the ambient temperature is 4 degrees Celsius, and the wind is blowing at 24 kilometres per hour, it will **FEEL LIKE** minus 5 degrees!

BRRRRRR!

FAST AND FURIOUS

Wind speed is measured with an **ANEMOMETER** and its strength with the **BEAUFORT SCALE**. At zero on the scale, there's no wind at all, so chimney smoke rises straight up into the sky. At 12, during a hurricane, both the chimney and the house it's attached to have probably blown away!

BEAUFORT WIND FORCE SCALE

Rating	Description
12	HURRICANE
11	VIOLENT STORM
10	STORM
9	STRONG GALE
8	GALE
7	NEAR GALE
6	STRONG WINDS
5	FRESH WINDS
4	MODERATE WINDS
3	GENTLE BREEZE
2	LIGHT BREEZE
1	LIGHT AIR
0	CALM

METRES PER SECOND

FAMOUS AUSSIE WINDS

During the summer months in Western Australia, a sea breeze called the **FREMANTLE DOCTOR** blows in off the Indian Ocean, cooling down Perth and Fremantle.

On the other side of the country, the **SOUTHERLY BUSTER** swoops in off the Pacific Ocean on sweltering summer afternoons, bringing cooling relief to sweaty Sydneysiders.

The **BRICKFIELDER** is not so welcome. This hot, dry wind rises in the deserts of Central Australia and blusters its way down to South Australia, causing day after day of searing temperatures.

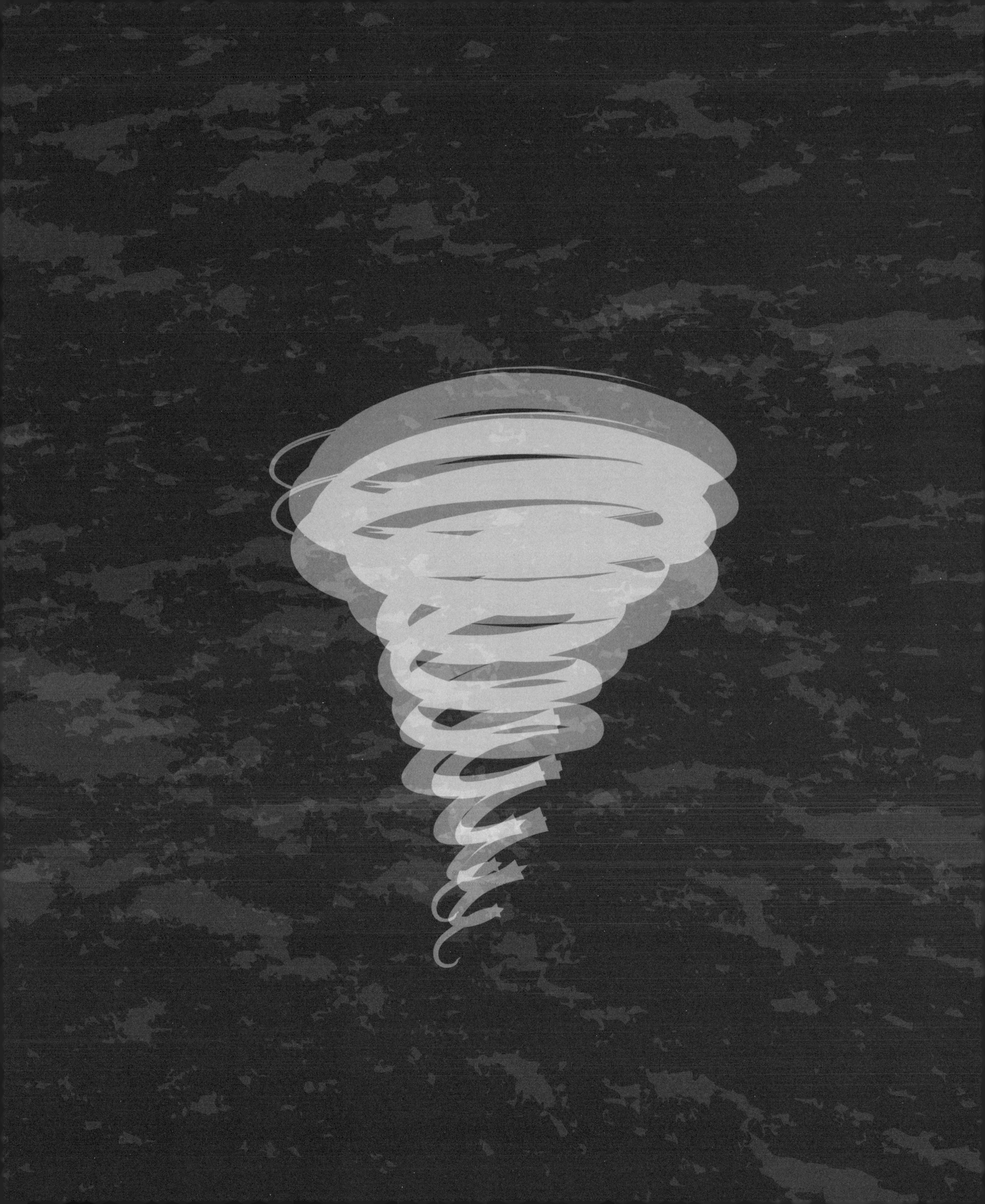

Disastrous Weather

Such was the tempest's great wrath, its violent strength, that one survivor told of seabirds falling dead on the decks of stricken pearling craft, their feathers torn from their bodies.

JIM McJANNETT, TORRES NEWS (THURSDAY ISLAND), 2008

Rogue Weather

Australia is a land of contrasts, plagued by floods and bushfires, cyclones and droughts. The acceleration of CLIMATE CHANGE, fuelled by human activities, is contributing to the number and intensity of these weather-related DISASTERS.

FATAL FIRES

In 1939, the BLACK FRIDAY bushfire burnt out 2 million hectares of land and killed 70 people in Victoria. At the height of the ASH WEDNESDAY bushfires in 1983, 180 fires burnt across Victoria and South Australia, taking the lives of 75 people. The BLACK SATURDAY bushfire in 2009 was even more devastating, with 173 people killed and over 2,000 homes destroyed. The 2019/2020 BUSHFIRE season was even more widespread, long-lasting and destructive. It burnt out over 18 million hectares of land across Australia, destroying forests, national parks, homes and businesses. At least 30 people and an estimated one billion animals died in these fiery infernos.

During the 2019/2020 bushfires, CANBERRA experienced SMOKE HAZE so bad that it had the WORST AIR QUALITY of any capital city in the world

FIERY STORMS

The heat put out by extreme bushfires creates PYROCUMULONIMBUS CLOUDS, which bring violent winds, thunder and lightning but no rain. These FIRESTORMS spread by hurling burning embers up to 30 kilometres away. They can also create fiery TORNADOES.

FEROCIOUS FLOODS

In the HUNTER VALLEY FLOODS of 1955, 24 people were killed and over 5,000 homes flooded. Around 40,000 people were evacuated. The major FLOOD that hit Queensland, Victoria and New South Wales in late 2010 affected over 200,000 people and killed 33.

MILLENNIUM DROUGHT 2002

RAINFALL
- BELOW AVERAGE
- WELL BELOW AVERAGE
- LOWEST ON RECORD

DREADFUL DROUGHTS

During the FEDERATION DROUGHT (1895–1902), the Darling River ran dry and wheat crops failed. The MILLENNIUM DROUGHT (2001–2009) was one of the worst in recorded history. Adelaide's water supply almost ran out, vital wetlands dried up and many animals died of hunger and thirst.

In January 2011, floodwaters covered three-quarters of the state of Queensland!

ONE HELL OF A HAILSTORM

A **SUPERCELL THUNDERSTORM** over Sydney in April 1999 created the **WORST HAILSTORM** and the most expensive **DISASTER** ever in Australia. Over 20,000 homes, 400,000 vehicles and 25 aeroplanes were damaged by hailstones the size of cricket balls. It cost a massive $2.3 billion to clean up the mess!

DARWIN ★

CHRISTMAS CALAMITY

Early on Christmas Day 1974, **CYCLONE TRACY** descended on Darwin. It killed 65 people and damaged or **DESTROYED** most of the city's buildings. More than half the people of Darwin were left homeless and had to be evacuated.

In March 2006, **CYCLONE LARRY** destroyed 80% of Australia's banana crop and $15 million worth of avocados

CATASTROPHIC CYCLONE

In 1899, **CYCLONE MAHINA** devastated Bathurst Island in Far North Queensland, killing over 400 people and almost destroying the pearling fleet. It was the most intense tropical cyclone **EVER** in the Southern Hemisphere. **DOLPHINS** were plucked from the sea by the storm surge it created and deposited on top of 15-metre-high cliffs!

Extreme Australia

Australia is prone to EXTREME WEATHER, from steaming heatwaves to teeming downpours, blustering winds and damaging hail. The Bureau of Meteorology keeps track of these wild and wonderful weather RECORDS.

2019 was the HOTTEST and DRIEST year on record in Australia

DARWIN
STRONGEST WIND IN A CAPITAL: 217km/h, Cyclone Tracy, 25 December 1974
HIGHEST AVERAGE ANNUAL RAINFALL IN A CAPITAL: 1,727mm
HIGHEST AVERAGE SUMMER TEMPERATURE IN A CAPITAL: 32°C

MARBLE BAR
HIGHEST AVERAGE MONTHLY MAXIMUM TEMPERATURE: 41.5°C in December
LONGEST HOT SPELL: 160 days over 37.8°C, 31 October 1923 to 7 April 1924

ULURU
MOST UNUSUAL SNOWFALL: 11 July 1997

OODNADATTA
HIGHEST MAXIMUM TEMPERATURE: 5 2 January 1960

In Central Australia, rocks can absorb enough HEAT to fry an egg!

PERTH
WINDIEST CAPITAL: winds average 15.6km/h
SUNNIEST CAPITAL: 8.8 hours of sunshine per day

EYRE
GREATEST TEMPERATURE RANGE IN ONE DAY: 6.8°C to 44.2°C 5 March 2008

The heat generated by a BUSHFIRE can melt cars and playground equipment

ADELAIDE
DRIEST CAPITAL: under 500mm of rain per year
HOTTEST TEMPERATURE FOR A CAPITAL: 46.6°C, January 2019

VICTORIA
WORST SINGLE-EVENT BUSHFIRE: Black Saturday, February 2009

LAKE MARGARET
MOST DAYS OF RAIN: 237 days per year

CAPE YORK PENINSULA
DEADLIEST AND MOST INTENSE CYCLONE: Cyclone Mahina, 1899

BUTTERFLIES can't flutter their wings when the weather's too cold

NORTH QUEENSLAND
COSTLIEST CYCLONE: Cyclone Yasi, 2011, $3.6 billion

BELLENDEN KER
HIGHEST ANNUAL RAINFALL: 12,461mm, 2000

TULLY
WETTEST TOWN: average annual rainfall 4,000mm

The highest **WIND SPEED** ever recorded was 408km/h at **BARROW ISLAND**, off Western Australia, in 1995

CLONCURRY
LONGEST NUMBER OF DAYS OVER 40°C: 33 days, from 16 December 2018 to 17 January 2019

QUEENSLAND

BRISBANE
WETTEST MONTH IN A CAPITAL: 1,026mm, February 1893
COSTLIEST FLOOD: December 2010 to January 2011, $2.38 billion

LAKE EYRE/ KATI THANDA
DRIEST PLACE: 125mm of rain per year

CROHAMHURST
HIGHEST RAINFALL IN 24 HOURS: 3 February 1893, 907mm

NEWCASTLE
WINDIEST CITY: average 32km/h

NEW SOUTH WALES

SYDNEY
COSTLIEST DISASTER: 1999 hailstorm, $2.3 billion

SOUTH AUSTRALIA

CHARLOTTE PASS
LOWEST MINIMUM TEMPERATURE: −23°C, 29 June 1994

CANBERRA
FOGGIEST CAPITAL: 47 fogs per year
COLDEST TEMPERATURE FOR A CAPITAL: −10°C, July 1971

VICTORIA

AUSTRALIAN CAPITAL TERRITORY

MELBOURNE
CLOUDIEST CAPITAL (YEARLY): 180 cloudy days per year

HOBART
CLOUDIEST CAPITAL (DAILY): 6.4 hours of sunshine
HIGHEST AVERAGE RAINY DAYS FOR A CAPITAL: 160 days
WINDIEST PLACE IN A CAPITAL: 174km/h, kunanyi/Mount Wellington

TASMANIA

Weatherproofing

Climate change is causing more EXTREME WEATHER in Australia, so it's important to make sure that both you and your home are as WEATHERPROOF as possible. If disaster does strike, stay safe by listening to experts—the police, the fire brigade and your STATE EMERGENCY SERVICE (SES).

DRESSING UP

DRESS SENSIBLY for the weather to avoid getting saturated, overheated or FROZEN stiff.

RAIN

HEAT

COLD

The iconic DRIZA-BONE coat and AKUBRA hat have been protecting Australians from the weather for over 100 years

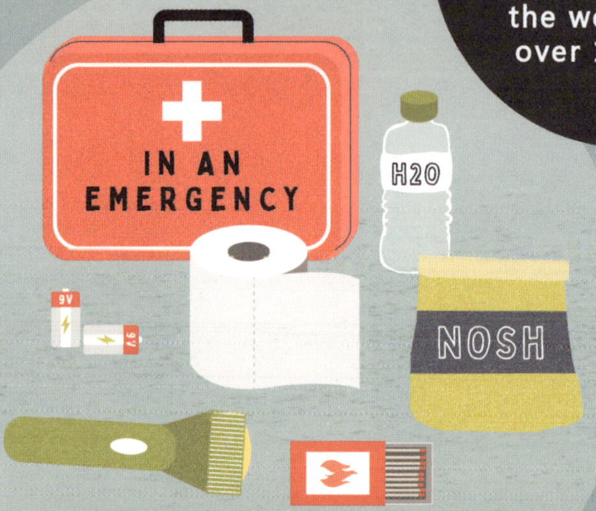

IN AN EMERGENCY

H20

NOSH

PROTECTIVE CLOTHING

During extreme weather, it's best to wear PROTECTIVE CLOTHING or stay safe indoors.

APPROVED FACE MASK

CLOSE-FITTING CLOTHING

BUSHFIRE

STORM

PUT ON YOUR PYJAMAS AND STAY INDOORS!

FLOOD

KEEP-SAFE KIT

In case of a WEATHER DISASTER, experts recommend you have an EMERGENCY KIT that includes a radio, torch, spare batteries, first-aid kit, toilet paper, candles, matches, snack food, drinking water and PROTECTIVE CLOTHING.

LET IT SNOW!

In alpine areas, steep roofs on houses and chalets stop **SNOW** piling up and breaking roof tiles. Footings built below the frost line and heavy-duty building materials help these houses withstand ice and snow. Good seals and **INSULATION** block out wintery chills and keep everyone snug and dry.

BIRDS build their nests inside bushes or on the leeside of trees to help protect them from storms

ANTI-ZAPPING DEVICES

Copper or aluminium **LIGHTNING RODS** are attached to the tops of buildings. When a lightning strike hits the rod, its **ELECTRICITY** is conducted down into the ground and safely absorbed, instead of zapping the building.

WATER, WATER EVERYWHERE

River **LEVEES** help prevent water overflowing into a town during a **FLOOD**. **SANDBAGS** help protect homes, shops and businesses if the levees are breached. **STORMWATER DRAINS** and other waterways are particularly dangerous during a flood, as pets, people and cars can be quickly swept away.

SAFE AS HOUSES

Houses can be weatherproofed to make them more comfortable to live in or to **PROTECT** them from extreme weather. For example, **QUEENSLANDERS** are built on stilts to let cooling breezes waft under, around and through them in hot, humid weather.

BUSHFIRE READY

When **BUSHFIRES** threaten, help protect your home by cleaning the gutters, pruning trees, mowing the lawn and cleaning up rubbish. **FIRE-RESISTANT** timber decks, shutters and roller doors make it harder for your house to catch fire.

WEATHERING THE STORM

To survive wild winds and teeming rain, **CYCLONE-PROOF** houses in northern Australia have multi-angled roofs, deep foundations, bolted doors, waterproof **SEALS** and shatterproof windows covered with shutters.

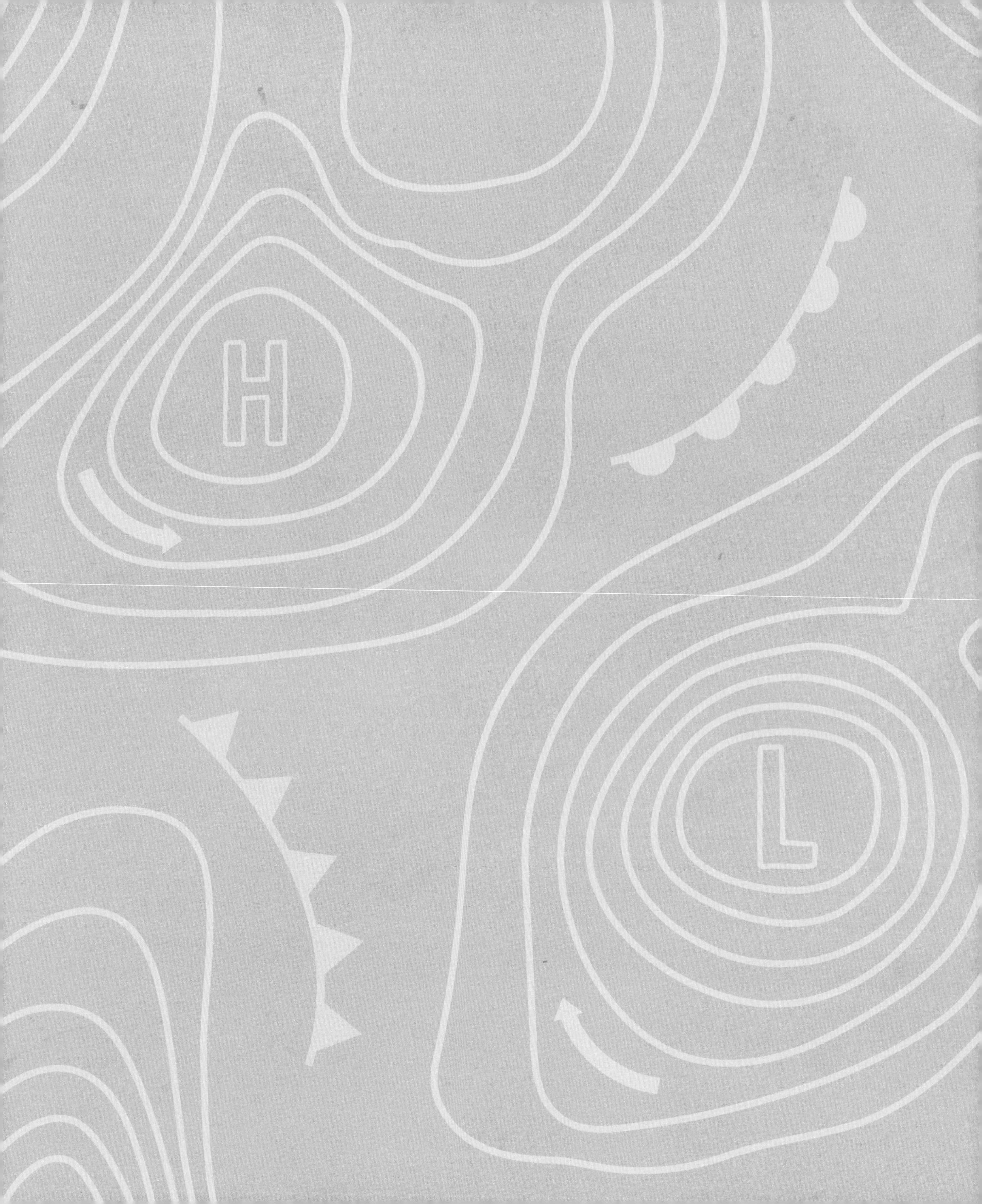
H
L

Weather Forecasting

Spiders are very intelligent weather experts ...
If it is going to rain, the spider promptly
shortens the long threads which support
his web. If it is going to be hot and fine
he lengthens them, thus enabling him
to take a sun bath more easily.

'CUB REPORTER' BETTY WILSON, AGED 9
THE AGE (MELBOURNE), 1937

Animal Antics

Over the centuries, people have used the BEHAVIOUR of ANIMALS to predict the weather. Some believe that when a cat sneezes, it's going to rain! We can't prove this, but many other animals do appear to be weather SENSITIVE.

BEASTLY BEHAVIOUR
Some animals can SENSE the drop in air pressure and rise in humidity before a storm. Farmers say that COWS often lie down before it rains—presumably so they'll have dry grass to eat when the rain stops. Insects are particularly vulnerable to wind and rain, so it's not surprising that BEES return to their hives when a storm is coming.

NOISY FROGS
FROGS need fresh water to lay eggs and produce tadpoles. So it makes perfect sense that they CROAK LOUDLY to attract a mate when rain is on its way!

CAMELS have closable nostrils and an extra pair of transparent eyelids to stop sand getting up their noses and in their eyes during a SANDSTORM

SAVVY SHARKS
SHARKS have such acute hearing that they can detect changes in the air pressure when a CYCLONE or a tropical storm is brewing. They swim into deeper water to stay safe.

TIME TO DIVE!

DEFYING THE DROUGHT
DROUGHT is part of the natural climate rhythm in Australia, so many native animals can cope with its harsh conditions. **BURROWING FROGS** hibernate deep under dried-up waterholes, emerging only when rain comes. The **ANTECHINUS**, or marsupial mouse, stores fat in its tail so it can survive the hard times.

NOT-SO-SILLY SHEEP
SHEEP snuggle together for protection when a **STORM** is coming, making one big woolly blanket. Some farmers say, 'When sheep gather in a huddle, tomorrow we'll have a puddle'.

PREDICTIVE PLANTS
PLANTS can also **PREDICT** the weather. In pine forests, ripe **PINE CONES** open up on dry days to shed their seeds, but close when the weather is humid and rain is on the way. **SEAWEED** washed up on a beach will be dry and brittle when the humidity is low, but damp and flexible when it's high.

SENSIBLE SEAGULLS
SEAGULLS are sensitive to changes in barometric pressure. When the pressure **DROPS** and a storm is coming, they seek shelter on the land. Other **SEABIRDS** fly low over the water, while land birds hide in trees.

Measuring Up

METEOROGLOGISTS use many **TOOLS** to measure weather patterns. Some, like the thermometer and the rain gauge, have been around for hundreds of years. Others are modern inventions.

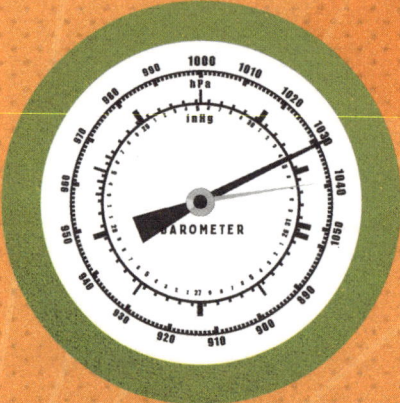

UP OR DOWN?

A **BAROMETER** measures atmospheric pressure—the weight of the air when it pushes against the ground. When the air is heavy with moisture, the **PRESSURE FALLS**, bringing stormy weather. When the air is dry, the pressure rises and the weather is fine.

UP, UP AND AWAY!

Helium-filled **WEATHER BALLOONS** carry instruments high into the sky. A small onboard weather station, called a **RADIOSONDE**, measures atmospheric pressure, temperature and humidity. It can also track and measure **WINDS**.

HELIUM BALLOON

The Bureau of Meteorology has over 700 **AUTOMATIC WEATHER STATIONS** scattered around Australia, and a few in Antarctica

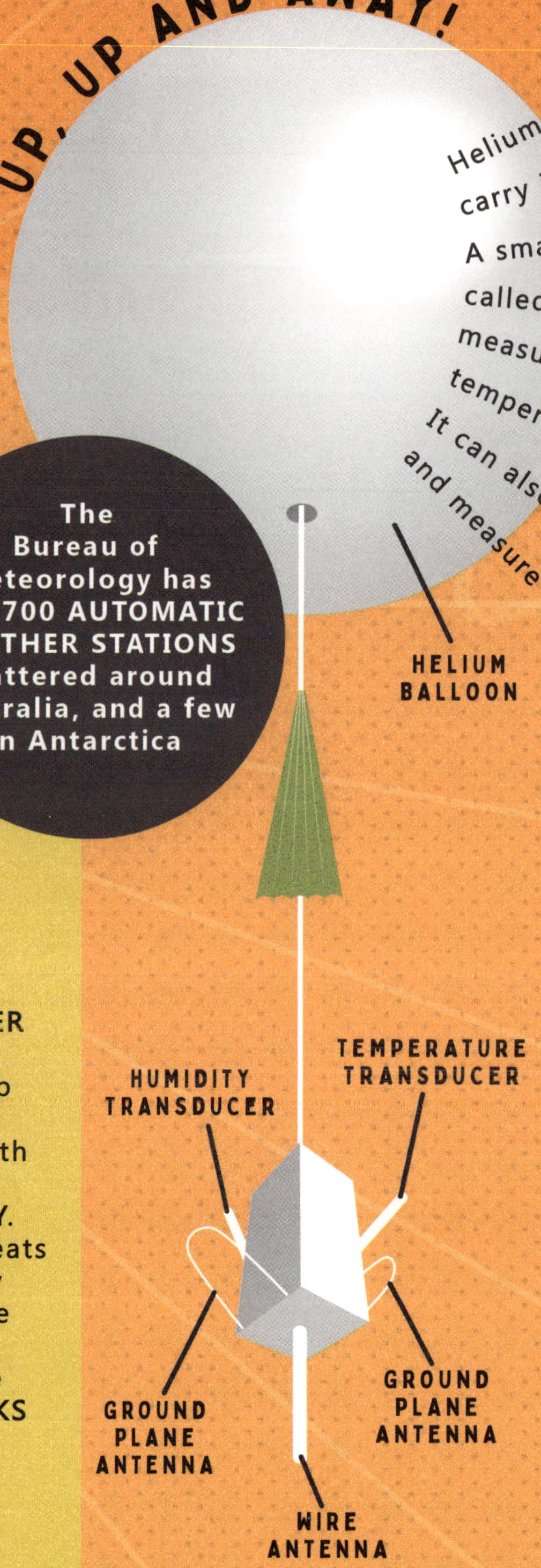

HUMIDITY TRANSDUCER
TEMPERATURE TRANSDUCER
GROUND PLANE ANTENNA
GROUND PLANE ANTENNA
WIRE ANTENNA

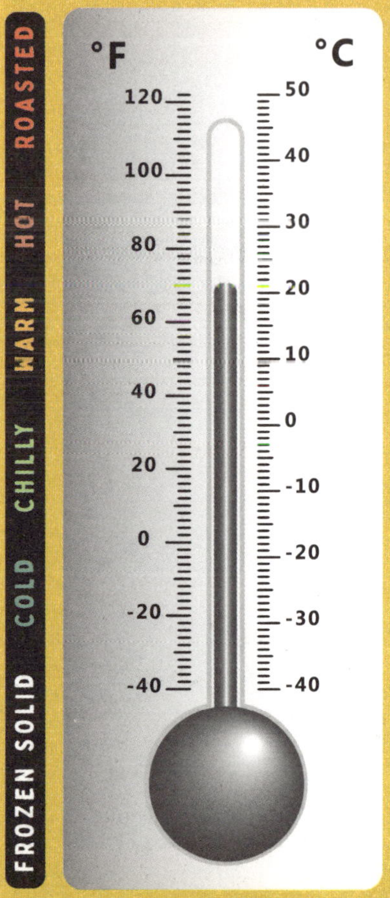

HOT AND COLD

A **THERMOMETER** has a fine glass tube with a bulb at the end. The bulb is filled with a liquid metal called **MERCURY**. When the air heats up, the mercury **EXPANDS** up the tube. As the air cools down, the mercury **SHRINKS** back towards the bulb.

FROZEN SOLID · COLD · CHILLY · WARM · HOT · ROASTED

READING UP A STORM

RADARS send radio waves up into the **SKY**. When these signals hit a rain or snow storm, they send an **ECHO** back to the radar, which then tracks the progress of the storm and measures its intensity.

LET IT POUR!
A RAIN GAUGE is a glass or plastic tube for collecting and measuring rain. A PLUVIOGRAPH is a more complicated rain gauge. It is used at WEATHER STATIONS to measure the amount and intensity of rainfall.

AWAY SHE BLOWS!
WINDVANES, WEATHERCOCKS and WINDSOCKS are used to measure the DIRECTION from which the wind is blowing—north, south, east or west, and all points in between.

HAIR-RAISING WEATHER
HUMIDITY is the amount of moisture in the air. It is measured using a HYGROMETER. A human or horse hair inside the device shrinks or expands as it absorbs moisture. The more moisture in the air, the more the hair expands. This helps explain why curly hair goes FRIZZY on a humid day!

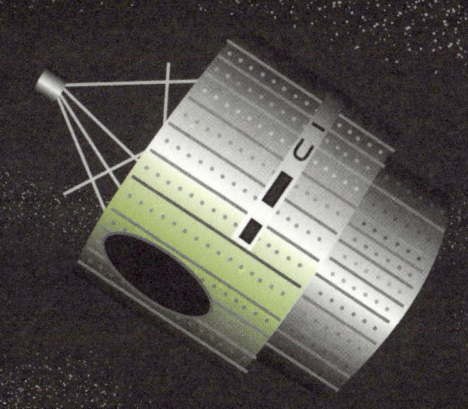

WHAT THE ...?

EYE IN THE SKY
METEOROLOGICAL SATELLITES orbit the Earth taking photographs. They provide information about humidity, temperature and wind, as well as cloud, snow and ice cover. Meteorologists use SUPERCOMPUTERS to analyse this information.

A CUP FULL OF WIND
ANEMOMETERS measure how fast the wind is blowing. The wind is caught in special cups attached to spinning poles. The WIND SPEED is measured by a computer run by a solar panel on an automatic weather station.

AHOY, MATEY!
High-tech FLOATING ROBOTS measure OCEAN TEMPERATURES. Ships and oil rigs also collect weather information far out at sea.

ARGO FLOAT

43

Reading the Weather

WEATHER FORECASTS are everywhere—in newspapers and smartphone apps, and on the radio, television and internet. It's very easy to find a weather REPORT, but it's only useful if you can interpret the information.

BURNING RAYS

The UV INDEX shows the level of ULTRAVIOLET RADIATION in the air. The higher the rating, the more likely you are to get badly sunburnt and be at risk of developing skin cancers. If the UV Index is above three, even on a cloudy or cool day, cover up or stay INDOORS!

MAGIC METEOROLOGISTS

Scientists who study, measure and forecast weather are called METEOROLOGISTS, while CLIMATOLOGISTS study changes in climate over time. On television, WEATHER PRESENTERS forecast the weather based on information from the Bureau of Meteorology.

UV INDEX

0–2	3–5	6–7	8–10	11+
LOW	MEDIUM	HIGH	VERY HIGH	EXTREME
sunscreen sunglasses	sunscreen sunglasses hat	sunscreen sunglasses hat shade	sunscreen sunglasses hat shade	sunscreen sunglasses hat shade stay indoors 10am to 4pm

When ANTS scurry hither and thither, reorganising their nests, RAIN may be on the way!

DANCING IN THE RAIN

In ANCIENT TIMES, people relied on plant and animal behaviour to help predict the weather. Sometimes they conducted ceremonies, such as RAIN DANCES, to try to change or control it.

TOOLS OF THE TRADE

It was not until the 1600s, when the THERMOMETER and BAROMETER were invented, that it was possible to accurately predict changes in the weather by measuring TEMPERATURE and AIR PRESSURE.

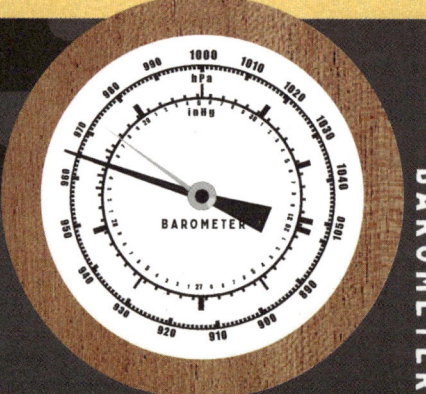

TIWI ISLANDS

FRONTING UP
A curved line of half-circles approaching a particular area on a weather map indicates a **WARM FRONT**, bringing clear skies and fine weather. A curved line of triangles indicates that a **COLD FRONT** is on the way, bringing clouds and rain.

COMING UP...
MAPPING THE WEATHER
Icons and symbols on **WEATHER MAPS** show what the weather will be. Curving lines called **ISOBARS** link areas with similar air pressure. Lines drawn close together indicate a **LOW PRESSURE** area, while lines drawn further apart indicate a **HIGH PRESSURE** area.

Meteorologists are fascinated by **HECTOR THE CONVECTOR**, a storm cloud that builds up around three o'clock every afternoon over the **TIWI ISLANDS**

WARM FRONT

MOVING AIR
In the Southern Hemisphere, **LOWS** (L) move clockwise and **HIGHS** (H) anticlockwise.

COLD FRONT

ICONIC WEATHER
Meteorologists include special **ICONS** on weather maps. They represent the forecast **WEATHER** and allow you to see at a glance whatever is coming your way.

The changes in **AIR PRESSURE** that affect our weather are measured in **MILLIBARS**

SUNNY · RAIN · CLOUDY · WINDY · SNOW

STORMS · HAIL · SHOWERS · SMOKE HAZE · FOG

45

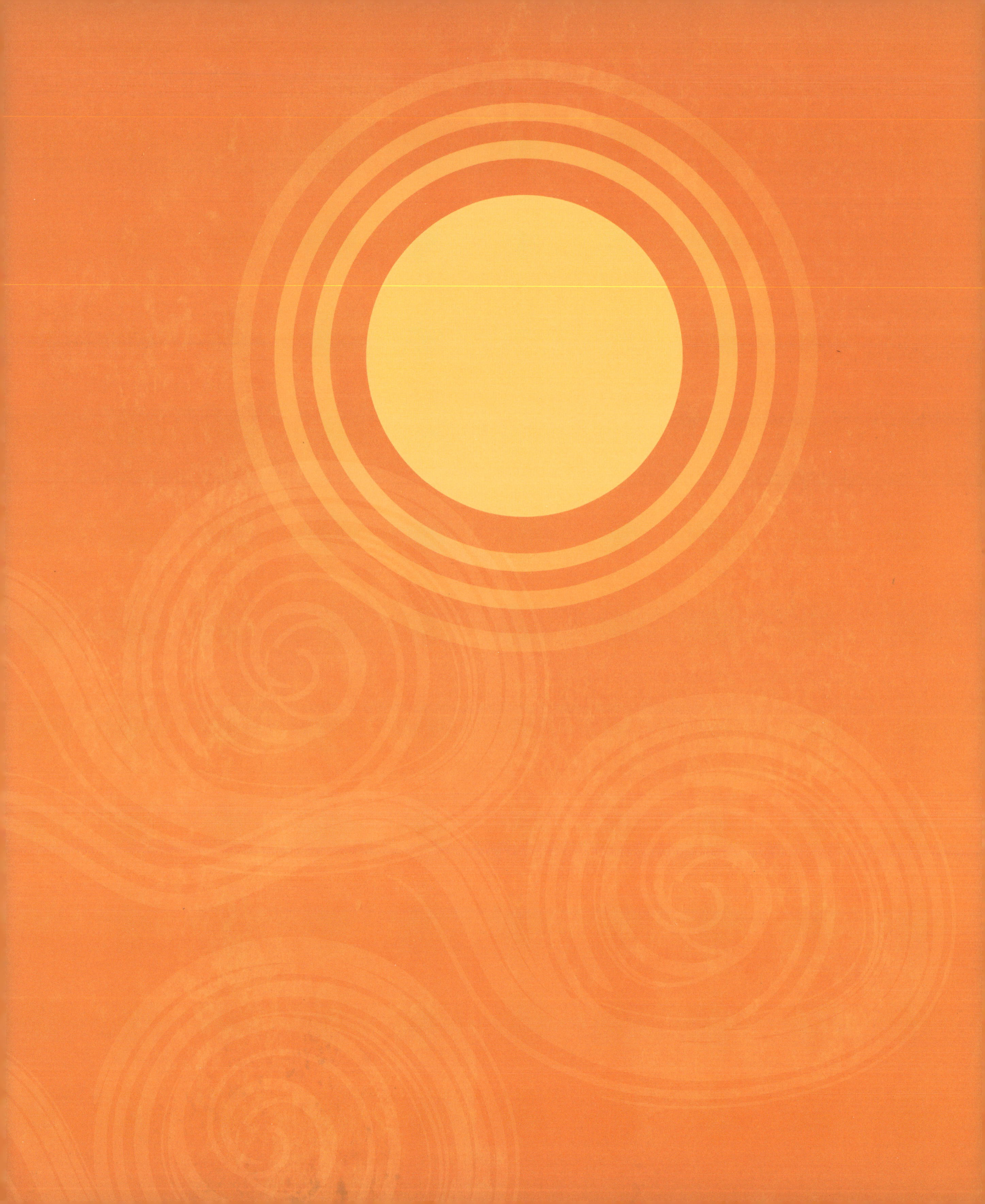

Climate Change

The Director of the Museum of Technology and Applied Sciences ... said that the Sydney climate was becoming hotter. The change had been most marked in the past two decades, but had been going on for the past 100 years.

THE COURIER-MAIL (BRISBANE), 1950

A Warming World

The Earth's climate has undergone natural cycles of warming and cooling for millions of years. In the past, these changes happened over thousands of years. Now, the rate of **CLIMATE CHANGE** is speeding up. Factories, power stations, motor vehicles and other sources of pollution send high levels of **GREENHOUSE GASES** into the air. This is affecting the delicate balance of gases in the atmosphere and causing **GLOBAL WARMING**.

NAUGHTY BOY

Australia's climate is influenced by the **SOUTHERN OSCILLATION INDEX**—the warming winds and waters of **EL NIÑO** (the boy child) and the cooling effects of **LA NIÑA** (the girl child). With climate change, El Niño is hanging out in Australia for longer, causing reduced rainfall, warmer temperatures and more **EXTREME** weather.

COASTAL CALAMITIES

POLAR ICE CAPS regulate the world's temperature. But the ice caps are melting, **RAISING SEA LEVELS**. It's predicted that, in the future, **FLOODING** will affect nearly half the people who live within 150 kilometres of the coast.

WARNING SIGNS

Nature provides many signs that **CHANGING WEATHER PATTERNS** are affecting the health of our planet. Oceans are **WARMING**, ice is **MELTING**, coral reefs—including the Great Barrier Reef—are being **BLEACHED** and many animals are at risk of extinction.

Sprinkler systems have been installed on some Queensland beaches to cool down the nests of **LOGGERHEAD TURTLES** so hatchlings don't die in the burning sand

PEOPLE POWER

POLLUTION produced by humans badly affects the weather and the climate. For example, **CHLOROFLUOROCARBONS** (CFCs) in air-conditioning, refrigerators, aerosol cans and solvents have damaged the protective **OZONE LAYER**. As this allows more dangerous ultraviolet light to reach the Earth's surface, CFCs are now banned.

OZONE LAYER

+10°C

CONCRETE JUNGLES

With their tall buildings, tar and cement, **CITIES** create their own **WEATHER SYSTEMS**. They can be up to 10 degrees Celsius warmer than the surrounding countryside, with its trees, grass and shrubs.

CORAL BLEACHING

GREENHOUSE EFFECT

The Earth's atmosphere acts like the glass walls and roof of a **GREENHOUSE**, absorbing the sun's warmth and using it to keep the Earth at a liveable temperature. Unfortunately, the burning of **FOSSIL FUELS** such as coal, oil and gas releases extra amounts of **CARBON DIOXIDE** into the atmosphere.

There is now more CARBON DIOXIDE in the air than at any time in the past three MILLION years

TOXIC WIND

When **COWS** eat grass, bacteria in their digestive systems produce the greenhouse gas **METHANE**. This gas is expelled into the atmosphere as **TOXIC FARTS**. The more cows we breed to feed people, the more methane is produced and the **HOTTER** the planet gets.

Learning from Nature

To prepare for the future, we need to understand and **LEARN** from the past. **CLIMATOLOGISTS** analyse hundreds of years of weather **RECORDS**. They also study the rings in tree trunks and core specimens taken from coral, ice sheets, glaciers and sediment at the bottom of lakes and oceans.

WEATHER LOGS

The rings in a **TREE TRUNK** are made by the new cells that grow in spring and summer. The width of each ring indicates how much the tree grew that year. That **GROWTH** depends on the weather—especially temperature and rainfall. The scientists who study tree rings are called **DENDROCLIMATOLOGISTS**. They can work out what the weather was like up to 4,000 years ago.

DANGEROUS DEFORESTATION

Trees are called the **LUNGS** of the Earth because they use up carbon dioxide and make life-giving **OXYGEN** during **PHOTOSYNTHESIS**. Cutting down established forests is called **DEFORESTATION**. It has devastating effects on the environment and leads to local changes in the weather, with hotter days and colder nights.

ONE YEAR

LESS WATER VAPOUR → FEWER CLOUDS → LESS RAIN → FEWER TREES → MORE CARBON DIOXIDE → LESS OXYGEN

During **PHOTOSYNTHESIS**, plants use sunlight to turn carbon dioxide into sugars, which they use for **ENERGY**

TODAY

ICY INFORMATION

Cores drilled through deep **ANTARCTIC ICE** can tell us what the climate was like up to 800,000 years ago. Each layer in an **ICE CORE** represents one year, and its thickness shows the amount of precipitation that year. Chemicals in the ice help scientists estimate the average temperatures of years past.

800,000 YEARS AGO

CORAL CATALOGUES

CORAL can live for centuries in a symbiotic relationship with the **ALGAE** that give them their colours. Scientists use X-rays to study the bands on slices of coral skeletons, which show **CHANGES** in the climate over time. Studies of corals in Australia reveal that there is a **LINK** between seasonal changes in rainfall and the surface temperature of the oceans.

CLIMATOLOGISTS collect weather information from the shells of fossilised **EMU EGGS** deposited up to 60,000 years ago at Lake Eyre/ Kati Thanda

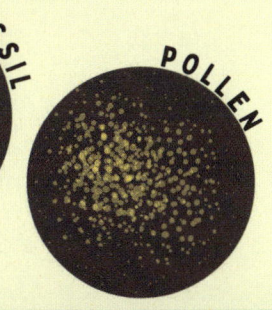

MOLLUSC FOSSIL

POLLEN

Acidification of the oceans is making it difficult for **MARINE CREATURES** to form solid **SHELLS** and **SKELETONS**—the **FOSSILS** of the future

UNDER WATER

Sediment at the bottom of **LAKES** and **OCEANS** provides climatologists with valuable information from hundreds of thousands of years ago. Preserved underwater in layers of rock and soil, animal **FOSSILS** and **POLLEN** from ancient plants show changes in ocean temperatures.

1,000 YEARS AGO

10,000 YEARS AGO

100,000 YEARS AGO

Weathering the Future

Scientists predict that the AVERAGE GLOBAL TEMPERATURE will rise by TWO to FOUR DEGREES CELSIUS in the next 100 years. That might not sound like a lot, but its effect will be significant, with warming oceans contributing to more extreme weather. Using renewable power sourced directly from nature—water, wind and sunlight—can help slow down this process.

CLEAN ENERGY

The **HILLS HOIST CLOTHES LINE** was invented in 1945 by Australian Lance Hill. It uses free energy from the **SUN** and **WIND** to dry clothes. It's a clean-energy alternative to your clothes dryer.

SOLAR POWER

Australia has more solar radiation per square metre than any other continent. **SOLAR PANELS** convert this energy into **ELECTRICITY**. Australia's first solar power station was set up in White Cliffs, New South Wales, in 1981. Today, there are **SOLAR FARMS** around the country, and many homes and businesses have roof-top solar panels.

HARNESSING HYDRO

Australia has been generating **ELECTRICITY** from water sources since the massive **SNOWY MOUNTAINS SCHEME** was finished in 1974. The proposed Snowy 2.0 could increase the capacity of the Snowy Mountains Scheme by 50 per cent. Tasmania is also ramping up its **HYDROPOWER** production, hoping to create what it calls the 'Battery of the Nation'.

WIND TURBINES

In 2019, around 20% of Australia's total energy came from **RENEWABLE SOURCES**. We MUST do better!

WIND is a relatively cheap source of renewable energy. The huge blades on **WIND TURBINES** capture the energy of the wind to generate electricity. **WIND FARMS** produce a third of Australia's clean energy.

BIOENERGY

BIOMASSES are burnt to generate electricity. In Queensland, burnt sugarcane waste fuels **THERMAL POWER** in sugar mills. **BIOFUELS** like ethanol are also produced from sugarcane and grain crops. Some cars use petrol blended with 10 per cent **ETHANOL**.

EARTH'S FURNACES

GEOTHERMAL ENERGY is extracted from natural heat sources deep **BENEATH** the Earth's surface. Potential sources have been identified in Central Australia, and **EXPLORATION** for geothermal sites is underway in all the states and the Northern Territory.

THERMAL ENERGY comes from molten rock called **MAGMA**, deep inside the Earth

CRUST
UPPER MANTLE
LOWER MANTLE
GRANITE
MAGMA
OUTER CORE

The superheated rock in the Earth's **MANTLE** makes up 84% of the planet's volume

INNER CORE

WAVE POWER

Australia is an island surrounded by surging surf, but there are no **WAVE-POWERED ENERGY** systems in full production—although a number are being **TESTED** in New South Wales, Western Australia and Tasmania.

Researching Weather

A subject which is always with us is the weather;
hot and hotter, cold and colder, wet and
wetter or dry and drier.

**DAILY COMMERCIAL NEWS
AND SHIPPING LIST (SYDNEY), 1938**

Exploring the Weather

The **NATIONAL LIBRARY OF AUSTRALIA** keeps its collections in a climate-controlled environment—nobody wants to read mouldy books! The Library also houses an impressive collection of material about the **WEATHER**. As well as books, newspapers, magazines and journals, there are maps, posters, charts, brochures, artworks, oral histories, photographs, cartoons, manuscripts and much more. It's a **TREASURE TROVE** of weather-related facts, figures, history, information and images. Here are just a few examples of what you can find in the Library's collections.

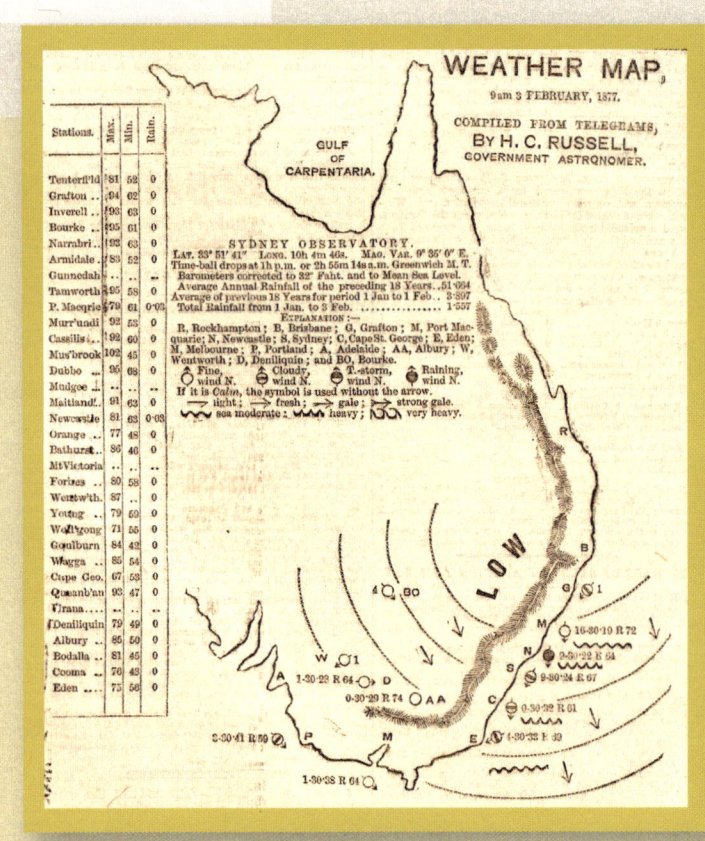

MAPPING THE WEATHER

The first published **WEATHER MAP** for the colony of New South Wales appeared in *The Sydney Morning Herald* on 5 February 1877. Produced by astronomer and meteorologist Henry Russell, it presented information gathered at the **SYDNEY OBSERVATORY** and at weather stations around the colony.

MEET THE METEOROLOGISTS

HENRY RUSSELL also invented instruments for measuring the weather. He loved his job so much that he often worked from nine in the morning until after midnight. Another colonial meteorologist, **CLEMENT WRAGGE**, produced almanacs. He upset local politicians he didn't like by naming **CYCLONES** after them. His stormy temper earned him the nickname 'Inclement' Wragge.

THE FIRST WEATHER MAP, 1877

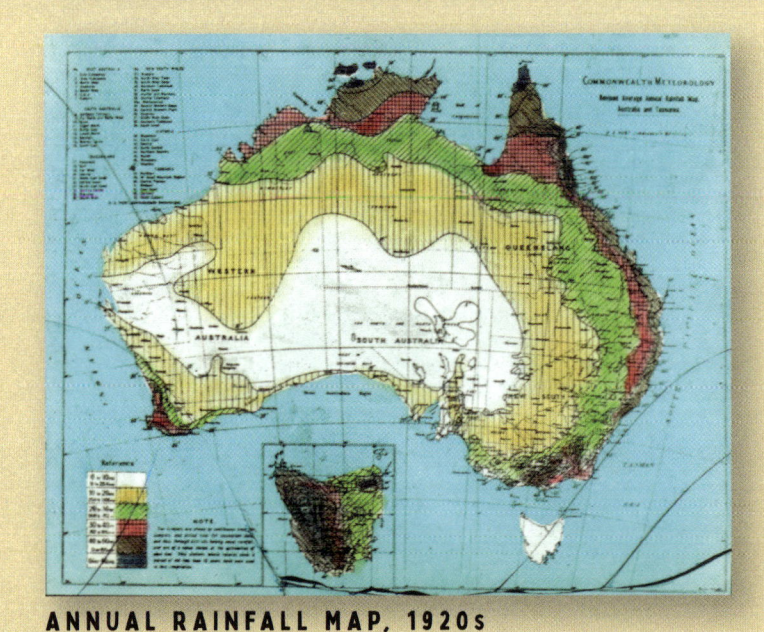

ANNUAL RAINFALL MAP, 1920s

SELF-RECORDING TIDE GAUGE, 1890s

INCLEMENT weather is unpleasant and stormy

INFORMATIVE ALMANACS

Weather information collected by colonial meteorologists was presented to the public in yearly **ALMANACS**. These useful books contained everything from weather forecasts to railway timetables, flags for signalling approaching storms and **HOUSEHOLD HINTS** for cleaning and cooking.

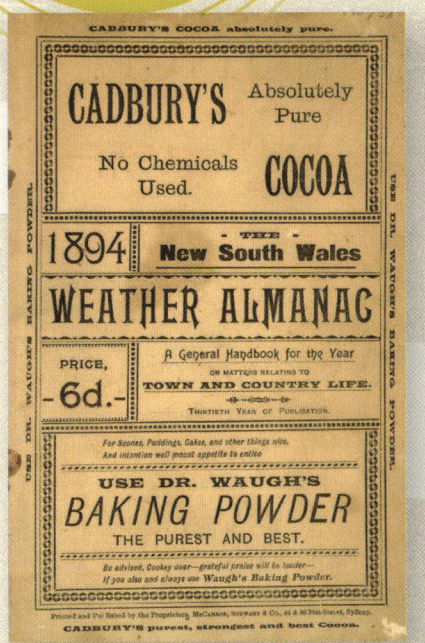

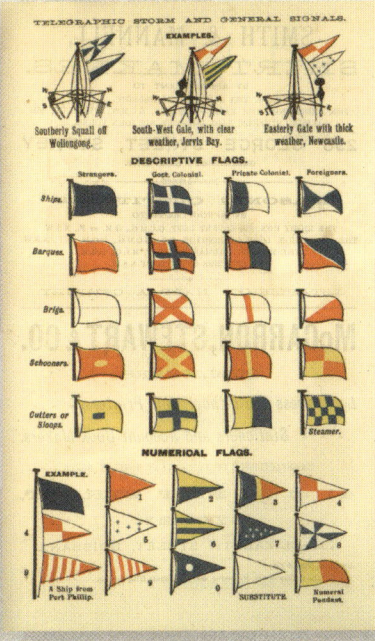

WEATHER ALMANAC FOR 1894

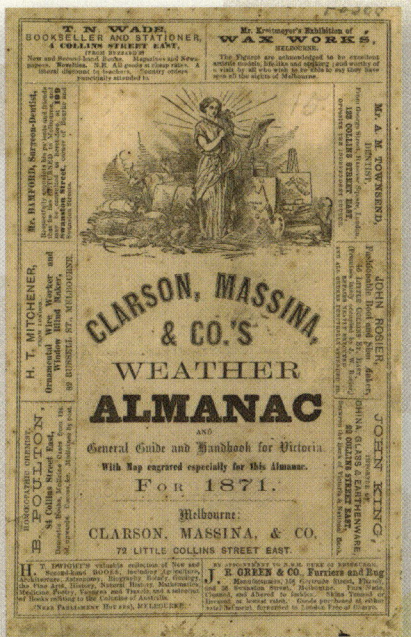

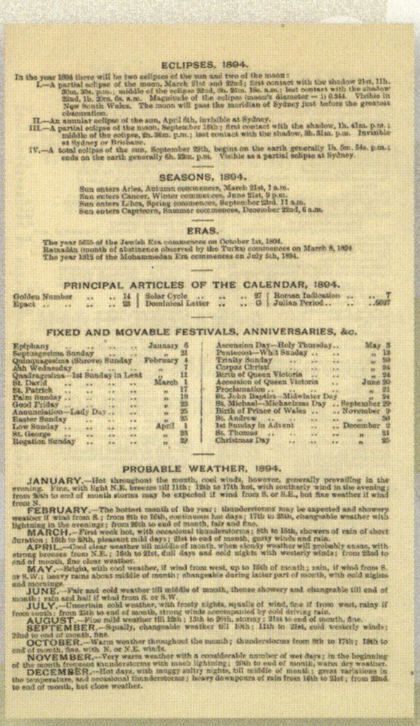

WEATHER ALMANAC FOR 1871

METEOROLOGICAL ADVENTURERS

Photographer **FRANK HURLEY** recorded the extraordinary life of **METEOROLOGISTS** exploring **ANTARCTICA** in the early 1900s. It is one of the windiest places on earth, and explorers were often blown off their feet in blizzards. Venturing outside could also lead to frostbite—and even death.

MEASURING THE TEMPERATURE, 1930s

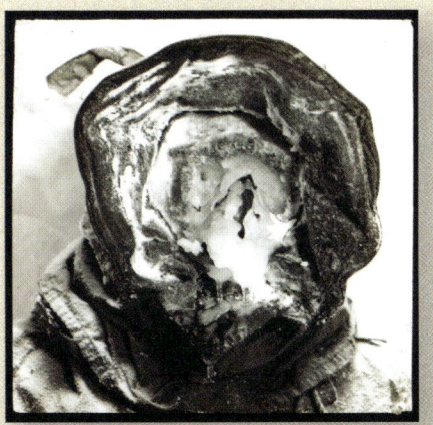

METEOROLOGIST CECIL MADIGAN, DURING AND AFTER A BLIZZARD, ANTARCTICA, 1910s

PAPER CHASE

'**EPHEMERA**' is a fancy name for everyday items such as flyers, bookmarks, badges and stickers. Weather-related ephemera includes postcards of flooded rivers and towns, newspaper cartoons, educational posters and wallcharts, and safety information brochures from the Bureau of Meteorology and state emergency services.

57

THE ART OF WEATHER

Weather is part of everyday life. People write **POEMS** and tell **STORIES** about it, and they draw and paint **PICTURES** depicting various aspects of the weather. They also compose weather-related **SONGS** and **MUSIC**, including musical renditions of Dorothea Mackellar's iconic poem about Australia and its weather, *My Country*.

A STORM ON THE GOLDFIELDS, 1850s

WILDLIFE ESCAPING A BUSHFIRE, 1850s

LIGHTNING MAN, 2003

A SNOWSTORM HITS HOBART, 1880s

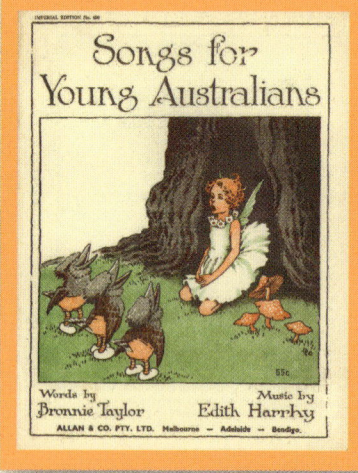

SONGS ABOUT THE WEATHER

DOCUMENTING DISASTERS

There are hundreds of thousands of **PHOTOS** of the major floods, bushfires, cyclones and droughts that have beset Australia since the 1800s. There are also **INTERVIEWS** with people who survived these disasters. Their stories provide insight into what it's like to experience **EXTREME WEATHER**.

MELTED SLIDE, CANBERRA, 2003

CYCLONE TRACY, DARWIN, 1974

> In the early hours of Christmas morning, in the pitch black of night, in the ruins of their homes, in the torrential rain and the shrieking gale, families huddled together under beds, in cupboards and anywhere that gave them a chance of survival.
>
> *Major General Alan Stretton describing CYCLONE TRACY, which hit the city of Darwin on 25 December 1974*

THE BOM'S AWAY!

The Australian **BUREAU OF METEOROLOGY (BOM)** was founded on 1 January 1908. It monitors the Earth's oceans and atmosphere to provide forecasts and weather reports. It also operates early-warning systems for **CYCLONES** and **TSUNAMIS**. Over the years, the bureau has produced everything from cloud charts and safety brochures to weather maps and storm-spotters' handbooks.

BOM BROCHURES

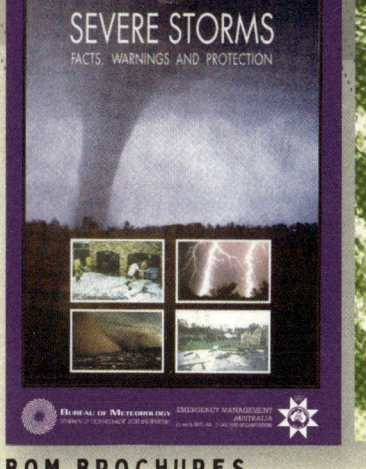

CHECKING OUT CLIMATE CHANGE

Scientists have known about greenhouse gases and global warming since the 1890s. Today, there is a lot more information on **CLIMATE CHANGE**, including scientific papers and academic books. Cartoons and ephemera from protests show how people have reacted to climate change. Photographs of the Australian landscape and its native plants and animals document the effects of warming sea temperatures, dying rivers, rising sea levels and melting ice caps.

MONITORING CORAL REEFS, 2005

WALK AGAINST WARMING, 2009

A CARTOON ON CLIMATE CHANGE, 2004

BUT WAIT, THERE'S MORE!

The information presented in *Australia's Wild, Weird, Wonderful Weather* was gathered from the collections of the **NATIONAL LIBRARY OF AUSTRALIA**. The photographs in this section of the book, as well as many of the images that inspired Tania McCartney's illustrations, also come from the Library. You can see some of this material online. Enter into your browser **catalogue.nla.gov.au** to search the Library's catalogue or **trove.nla.gov.au** to search newspapers and much more. You can also find more ways to explore the weather in the teachers' notes for this book at **publishing.nla.gov.au/pages/teachers-notes.do**.

Weather Words

A
acidification the process of becoming more acidic
air pressure the weight of the atmosphere over the Earth's surface
algae small plant-like organisms
almanac a book or calendar providing yearly weather information
alpine relating to mountains
altitude height above sea level
anemometer an instrument that measures wind speed
arid dry, hot and barren
atmosphere the layers of air surrounding the Earth
aurora electrically charged light display in the sky, usually near the south or north magnetic poles

B
barometer an instrument used for measuring air pressure
biofuel a fuel, such as ethanol, made from plants
biomass organic matter used to produce electricity
blizzard a snowstorm with high winds and whiteout conditions
breeze a gentle movement of air

C
calamities disasters
carbon dioxide a common gas in Earth's atmosphere that is needed by plants to survive
chlorofluorocarbons gases produced by industrial processes that deplete the ozone layer
climatologist a scientist who studies climates and climate change
convection upward movement of warm air that condenses to form rain clouds
cyclone a destructive tropical storm

D
deforestation the destruction of established or old-growth forests
dendroclimatology the study of tree rings to determine changes in climate over time
dew drops of moisture that form on low-lying surfaces overnight
drizzle light rainfall
drought a long period of abnormally low rainfall
dust devil a small whirlwind, usually in the desert

E
electron a subatomic particle that carries electricity
ephemera everyday items like postcards, badges and stickers
evaporate turn from a liquid into a gas or vapour

F
flammable easily set on fire
fog ground-level cloud
fossil fuel a source of energy obtained from under the Earth's surface, such as coal or gas
frost frozen dew, formed when the temperature is below zero degrees Celsius
frostbite injury to the skin caused by exposure to extreme cold

G
gale a very strong wind
gauge an instrument for measuring things like air pressure or rain
geothermal relating to the heat from the molten core of the earth
greenhouse effect an increase in the Earth's temperature caused by gases in the atmosphere trapping the sun's heat
greenhouse gases natural and artificial gases that trap the sun's heat on Earth

H
hail lumps of ice falling from thunderclouds
heatwave an extended period of higher-than-usual temperatures
hexagonal having six sides
hibernate hide away during periods of extreme heat or cold
hoarfrost deposits of ice crystals
humidity the amount of moisture in the air
hurricane a severe tropical storm
hydropower electricity produced by the movement of water
hygrometer a machine that uses horse or human hair to measure humidity in the air

I
icon a pictorial representation
inclement stormy
indigo deep violet blue
inundate flood
isobars lines on a weather map linking areas of equal air pressure

L

Latin the language of ancient Rome, often used for scientific names
leeside the side protected from the wind
lightning a giant spark of electricity

M

mackerel a fish
mantle the layer of the Earth just below the crust
meteor a small body of matter passing through the Earth's atmosphere, a shooting star
meteorologist a scientist who studies atmospheric conditions in order to forecast the weather
meteorology the science of studying atmospheric conditions, especially relating to weather
mist thin, ground-level cloud
moisture water vapour in the air
monolith a single large stone object, such as Uluru
monsoon the rainy season

O

optical illusion something that deceives the eye
oxygen a common gas in the atmosphere necessary for life on Earth
ozone a form of oxygen that absorbs ultraviolet light

P

phenomena strange, interesting or unusual weather events
photosynthesis the process by which plants convert light into food
pluviograph an instrument for measuring the volume and intensity of rainfall
pollution waste from human activity
precipitation moisture, whether liquid or solid, that falls from a cloud to the ground
prism an object that separates light into the colours of the spectrum

R

radiation emission of energy as electromagnetic rays
radiosonde a weather station attached to a balloon

S

savvy shrewd and knowledgeable
serein rain that falls from a blue sky; a sunshower
shower short-lived rainfall, either light or heavy, falling over a small area
sleet partly melted snow or frozen rain
snow large hexagonal ice crystals
solvent a cleaning fluid used for dissolving other substances
spectrum the band of colours produced by light passing through a prism
stratosphere the part of the Earth's atmosphere containing the ozone layer
supercell a slow-moving, rotating thunderstorm causing heavy rain, hail or tornadoes
supersonic above the speed of sound
superstorm a powerful and destructive storm
symbiosis a mutually beneficial relationship

T

temperate having a moderate temperature
thermal power electricity produced using heat
thermometer a tool for measuring temperature
thunder the sound created by lightning
tornado a violent, funnel-shaped whirlwind
transparent see-through
tsunami an enormous wave caused by an earthquake, volcanic eruption or landslide
twister a whirlwind or tornado
typhoon a tropical storm

U

ultraviolet a wavelength less than visible light

V

virga rain that falls from a cloud but doesn't make it to the ground

W

water vapour the moisture in the air
waterspout a whirlwind over the ocean or other body of water
whirlwind a mass of rotating air
whiteout heavy, low cloud cover and snowfall that makes the horizon invisible
willy-willy a spiralling wind
wind the flow of air over the surface of the Earth
windvane an instrument for showing wind direction, also called a weathercock or a weathervane

Weather Resources

BOOKLIST

Birch, Robin, *Weather and Climate: How Weather Works*. Melbourne: Macmillan Library, 2009.
Brasch, Nicolas, *Weather and Climate*. Melbourne: Echidna Books, 2005.
Burroughs, William J. et al., *An Australian Geographic Guide to Weather*. Sydney: Weldon Owen, 2004.
Butler, John E., *People and the Weather*. Melbourne: Longman Cheshire, 1981.
Colls, Keith and Whitaker, Richard, *The Australian Weather Book*. Sydney: Reed New Holland, 2012.
Crowder, Bob, *The Wonders of Weather*. Canberra: AGPS, 1995.
Day, David, *The Weather Watchers: 100 Years of the Bureau of Meteorology*.
    Melbourne: Melbourne University Publishing, 2007.
Elish, Dan. *Big Awesome Weather & Natural Disasters*. Bath, UK: Parragon, 2018.
Ellyard, David (ed.), *Discoveries: Weather*. Sydney: Weldon Owen, 1996.
Farndon, John, *Extreme Weather*. London: DK, 2007.
Healey, Justin, *Extreme Weather and Natural Disasters*. Sydney: Spinney Press, 2012.
Levinson, Cynthia, *What Will the Weather Be? All about Forecasting the Weather*.
    Melbourne: Macmillan Education Australia, 2018.
Macinnis, Peter, *Australian Backyard Earth Scientist*. Canberra: NLA Publishing, 2019.
McClish, Bruce, *Weather in Australia*. Melbourne: Macmillan Education Australia, 1998.
Pascoe, Bruce, *Young Dark Emu: A Truer History*. Broome, WA: Magabala Books, 2019.
Science in Our World: Weather. Melbourne: Macmillan Education, 1991.
Trafford, Caren and Wilsher, David, *Weather or Not ... It's a Climate for Change*. Sydney: Etram, 2007.
Wild, Ailsa and Reed, Aviva, *Zobi and the Zoox: A Story of Coral Bleaching*. Melbourne: CSIRO Publishing, 2018.

WEBSITES

Bureau of Meteorology: bom.gov.au
    Air quality: bom.gov.au/catalogue/warnings/air-pollution.shtml
    Cyclone names: bom.gov.au/cyclone/about/names.shtml
    Educational information: bom.gov.au/climate/data-services/education.shtml
    Heatwave information: bom.gov.au/australia/heatwave
    Indigenous seasonal calendars: bom.gov.au/iwk/calendars/gariwerd.shtml
    Indigenous weather knowledge: bom.gov.au/iwk
    Weather icons: media.bom.gov.au/social/blog/20/icons-what-do-they-mean-to-you
    Weather radar: bom.gov.au/australia/radar

State Emergency Services (SES):
    Australian Capital Territory: esa.act.gov.au/state-emergency-service
    New South Wales: ses.nsw.gov.au
    Northern Territory: pfes.nt.gov.au/emergency-service
    Queensland: ses.qld.gov.au/Pages/default.aspx
    South Australia: ses.sa.gov.au/site/home.jsp
    Tasmania: es.tas.gov.au
    Victoria: ses.vic.gov.au
    Western Australia: dfes.wa.gov.au/Pages/default.aspx

Extra Weather Information
    Drought: abc.net.au/news/2014-02-26/100-years-of-drought/5282030
    Emergency: abc.net.au/news/emergency
    Global warming: nationalgeographic.com/environment/global-warming/geothermal-energy
    Icicles: theglobeandmail.com/technology/science/the-mysterious-and-cool-science-of-icicles/article23241318
    Indigenous seasons: abc.net.au/btn/classroom/indigenous-seasons/10522128
    Kakadu seasons: parksaustralia.gov.au/kakadu/discover/nature/seasons
    Snow: rd.com/culture/fun-snow-facts
    Sun smart information: sunsmart.com.au

FROM THE NATIONAL LIBRARY COLLECTIONS

To listen to the oral history recordings or read the newspaper articles featured in this book, go to catalogue.nla.gov.au or trove.nla.gov.au/newspaper. To view the Library items featured here, enter **nla.gov.au/** followed by the item's catalogue identifier provided in the list of items below (e.g. nla.gov.au/nla.news-article158227133).

PAGE 7
'Floods', *The Gnowangerup Star and Tambellup-Ongerup Gazette*, 9 November 1940, p.2, nla.news-article158227133.

PAGE 14
'The Weather: Hail Storm', *The Yass Courier*, 13 December 1910, p.2, nla.news-article246632295.

PAGE 22
'Ball Lightning', *Daily Mercury*, 2 November 1953, p.10, nla.news-article169660249.

PAGE 30
Jim McJannett, 'The Great Cyclone Mahina and Tsunami and a Search for a Thursday Island Grave', *Torres News*, 6 August 2008, p.4, nla.news-article254355730.

PAGE 38
'Weather Prophets', *The Age*, 4 November 1937, p.17, nla.news-article205560442.

PAGE 46
'Climate Change: World is Warming', *The Courier-Mail* 22 May 1950, p.3, nla.news-article49734531.

PAGE 54
'Meteorological Research', *Daily Commercial News and Shipping List*, 5 August 1938, p.4, nla.news-article162055697.

PAGE 56
'Weather Map', page 6 in *The Sydney Morning Herald*, 5 February 1877, nla.news-article1438919; Henry Ambrose Hunt, *Revised Average Annual Rainfall Map, Australia and Tasmania*, 1920s, nla.cat-vn2154303; 'Self-recording Tide-gauge', opposite page 8 in *Meteorological Instruments* by Henry Chamberlain Russell, 1871–1904, nla.cat-vn520567.

PAGE 57
'1894', page 1 in *New South Wales Weather Almanac*, 1893, nla.cat-vn2213641; 'Telegraphic Storm and General Signals', page 4 in *New South Wales Weather Almanac*, 1893, nla.cat-vn2213641; *Clarson, Massina, & Co's Weather Almanac and General Guide and Handbook for Victoria*, 1871, nla.cat-vn677178; 'Australian Seasons 1894', page 7 in *New South Wales Weather Almanac*, 1893, nla.cat-vn2213641; *Assistant Meteorologist Mr. Finke Reading the Temperature on Thermometers at the Weather Bureau*, New South Wales, 1930s, nla.cat-vn6265315, courtesy The Sydney Morning Herald; Frank Hurley, *The Meteorologist with an Ice-mask*, Australasian Antarctic Expedition, c.1913, nla.cat-vn1550585; Frank Hurley, *Madigan's Frostbitten Face*, Adelie Land, Australasian Antarctic Expedition, c.1913, nla.cat-vn29174; 'Severe Weather: Facts and Warnings', c.1993, in *Weather: Ephemera Material Collected by the National Library of Australia*, nla.-cat-vn2600914, reproduced by permission of Bureau of Meteorology, © 2019 Commonwealth of Australia.

PAGE 58
George Lacy, *Moist Weather: Road to the Diggings*, c.1852, nla.cat-vn2583328; William Strutt, *Bush Fires in the Moorabbin District*, 1854, nla.cat-vn1228260; Harold John Graham, *Severe Snow Storm over Hobart*, 1882, nla.cat-vn909564; Paddy Wainburranga Fordham, *Lightning Man*, 2003, nla.cat-vn7579431, © Paddy Wainburranga Fordham/Copyright Agency, 2019; Harold John Graham, *Severe Snow Storm over Hobart*, 1882, nla.cat-vn909564; Ida Rentoul Outhwaite, cover of *Songs for Young Australians* by Edith Harrhy and Bronnie Taylor, c.1941, nla.cat-vn2798305, courtesy Vanessa Martin & Stella Palmer; Damian McDonald, *Damaged Playground Facility in Duffy, Canberra*, 2003, nla.cat-vn3064303; Alan Dwyer, *Houses Destroyed by Cyclone Tracy, Darwin* 1974, nla.cat-vn3112050; Stretton, Alan, *Alan Stretton Address to the National Press Club on 13 February 1975*, nla.cat-vn558762.

PAGE 59
'Severe Storms', c.1992, in *Bureau of Meteorology: Ephemera Material Collected by the National Library of Australia*, nla.cat-vn1077419, reproduced by permission of Bureau of Meteorology, © 2019 Commonwealth of Australia; 'Know Your Cyclone Warning System', 1983, in *Bureau of Meteorology: Ephemera Material Collected by the National Library of Australia*, nla.cat-vn1077419, reproduced by permission of Bureau of Meteorology, © 2019 Commonwealth of Australia; Simon O'Dwyer, *Marine Botanist Peter Ralph Surveys the Reef with a Fluorometer to Measure Stress Levels in Coral Algae, Heron Island*, 2005, nla.cat-vn4533099; Wendy McDougall, *Placards on Display during the Walk against Warming, Martin Place, Sydney*, 2009, nla.cat-vn4803267; Alan Moir, *Global Warming Is a Myth*, 2004, nla.cat-vn3639568.

Index

Page numbers in **bold** refer to illustrations and diagrams.

A

acidification, 51
Adelaide, 32, 34
aerials, 27, **28**
aeroplanes *see* planes
air pressure, 9, 18, 19, 40, 41, 42, 44, 45
Akubra hat, 36
algae, 51
almanacs, 56, 57, **57**
alpine areas, 20, 37
alyurr, 11, **11**
ambient temperature, 12, 29
ancestral beings, 11
anemometers, 29, 43, **43**
animal forecasting, 40–41, **40–41**
animals, 10, 11, 18 40–41
Antarctica, 42, 57
antechinus, 41, **41**
antennas, **42**
anti-cyclonic gloom, 16
ants, 44, **44**
apparent temperature, 12, 29
Arctic Circle, 24
argo floats, 43, **43**
argon, 8
Arnhem Land, 11
artwork, 56, 58, **58**
Ash Wednesday, 32
atmosphere, 8, **8–9**, 9, 18, 25, 48, 49
atmospheric pressure *see* air pressure
Aurora Australis, 24
auroras, 24, **24**
Australian Capital Territory, **35**
autumn, 8
avocadoes, 33, **33**

B

balloons, 42, **42, 59**
bananas, 33, **33**
barometers, 11, 42, **42**, 44, **44**
barometric pressure, 41
Barrow Island, 35
Bathurst Island, 33
Beaufort Scale, 29, **29**
bees, 11, **11**, 40, **40**
Bellenden Ker, 35
Bininj/Mungguy peoples, 8
bioenergy, 53
biofuel, 53
biomass, 53
birds, 11, **11**, 20, **37**, 41, **41**
black cockatoos, 11, **11**
Black Friday, 32
Black Saturday, 32
blizzards, 21, 28, 57
boats, 26, 28, **29**, 35
bogong moths, 24, **24**
boiling point, 12
BOM *see* Bureau of Meteorology
breezes, 28, 29, 39
Brickfielder, 29
Brisbane, 32, 35
buildings, 12, 27, **37**, 37, **46**, 49
Bureau of Meteorology, 9, 10, 12, 13, 26, 34, 42, 44, 57, 59
bushfires, 12, 25, 32, 34, 36, 37, 58, **58**
butterflies, 10, **10**, 35, **35**

C

Cairns, 13
calendars, 10–11
camels, 13, **13**, 40, **40–41**
Canberra, 32, 35, 58
canoes, 11, **11**
Cape York Peninsula, 35
carbon dioxide, 8, 49, 50
cars, 28, **28**, 32, 34, **34**, 37, **37**, 53
cartoons, 56, 57, 59, 59
cats, **27**, 40
Celsius, 12, 29
Central Australia, 10, 12, 13, 29, 34, 53
CFCs *see* chlorofluorocarbons
Charlotte Pass, 35
chimneys, 27, **27**, 28, 29
chlorofluorocarbons, 49, **49**
Christmas Day, 26, 33, 58
cities, 17, 49, **49**
climate, **8–9**, 9, 10, 41, 44, 48, 49, 51
climate change, 32, 36, 48–49, **48–49**, 50–51, **50–51**, 59
climatic zones, 8–9, **8–9**
climatologists, 44, 50, 51
Cloncurry, 35
clothes lines *see* Hills Hoist
clothing, **20**, 36, **36**
cloud seeding, 17, **17**
clouds, 9, 16–17, **16–17**, 18, 19, 21, 26, **27**, 32, 35, 45
cockatoos, 11, **11**
cold fronts, 28, 45, **45**
colour spectrum, 21, 24–25, **24–25**
coral, 48, 49, **48–49**, 50, 51, **51**, 59
coral bleaching, 49, **49**
cows, 16, **16**, 40, 49, **49**
cricket balls, 33, **33**
Crohamhurst, 35
Cyclone Larry, 33
Cyclone Mahina, 33, 35
Cyclone Tracy, 33, **33**, 34, 58, **58**
Cyclone Yasi, 35
cyclones, 28, 29, **29**, 32, 33, **33**, 34, 35, **35**, 37, 40, 56, 58, 59

D

Darling River, 32
Darwin, 26, 33, **33**, 34, 58
deforestation, 50, **50**
dendroclimatologists, 50
desert climate zone, 8–9, **8–9**
deserts, **8–9**, 10, 13, 18, 28, 29

dew, 18, 20
disasters, 32–33, **32–33**, 35, 36, 58
dolphins, 33, **33**
Dreaming stories, 11
drilling rigs, **53**
Driza-bone coat, 36
drizzle, 19
drought, 13, **13**, 17, 28, 32, **32**, 41, 58
dry season, 8
dust, 16, 17, 25, 28
dust devils, 28
dust storms, 28, **28**

E

Earth, **9**, **53**
eels, 11, **11**
El Niño, 48
electricity, 26, 37, 52–53, **52**
emergency kit, 36, **36**
emergency services, 36, 57
emu eggs, 51, **51**
ephemera, 57, **57**, 59, **59**
equator, 9
equatorial climate zone, 8–9, **8–9**
ethanol, 53
extreme weather, 32–33, **32–33**, 34–35, 36, 37, 48, 52, 58
Eyre, 34

F

Fahrenheit, 12
Federation Drought, 32
fire see bushfires
fire danger rating, **12**
firestorms, 32
fish, 13, 17, 19, **19**, 43
flags, 57, **57**
floods, 11, **11**, 19, 32, **32**, 35, 36, 37
flying foxes, 13, **13**
fog, 17, 24, 35
fogbows, 24, **24**
forecasting, 10–11, **10–11**, 40–41, **40–41**, 42–43, **42–43**, 44–45, **44–45**, 57, 59
fossil fuels, 49
fossils, 51, **51**
freezing point, 12, **12**

Fremantle Doctor, 29
frogs, 19, **19**, 40, **40**, 41
frost, 20, 37
frostbite, 20, 29, 57, **57**

G

gales, 28
Gariwerd calendar, 10, **10–11**
gases, 8, 24, 48, 49
geothermal energy, 53
gidgee, 11, **11**
glaciers, 28, 50
global warming, 48–49, **48–49**, 59
Goorialla, 11
Grampians, 10, 11
granite, **53**
grasshoppers see alyurr
grassland climate zone, 8–9, **8–9**
Great Barrier Reef, 48
Great Victoria Desert, 13, **13**
greenhouse effect, 49, **49**
greenhouse gases, 49, **49**, 59
Gundagai, 11
gusts, 28, 29

H

hail, 15, 18, 20, 21, **21**, 33, **33**, 34, 35
hailstorms, 33, 35
halo, 18
hamburgers, 18, **18**
heat, 12–13, **12–13**
heatwaves, 12, 13, 34
Hector the Convector, 45
high pressure system, 28, **44**, 45
Hill, Lance, 52
Hills Hoist, 52, **52**
hoarfrost, 20
Hobart, 35, 58
horses, 17, 28, **29**, 43, **43**
houses, **27**, 28, **32**, 37, **37**, 58
humidity, 11, 12, 13, 19, 40, 41, 42, 43, **43**
Hunter Valley, 32
Hurley, Frank, 57
hurricanes, 28, 29
hydropower, 52, **52**
hygrometer, 43
hypothermia, 20

I

ice, 20–21, **20–21**, 37, 43, 48, **48**, 50, 51, **51**
ice blocks, **12**, 56
ice caps, 48, **48**, 59
ice cores, 51, **51**
ice crystals, **16**, 17, 21, 26
ice gardens, 20, **20**
ice sheets, 50–51
icicles, 20, **20**
icons, **8**, **14**, **19**, **20**, **22**, **30**, **32**, **34**, **35**, **37**, **38**, 44, **44**, 45, **45**, **46**, 54, **54**
Indian Ocean, 29
Indigenous Australians, 8, 10–11
Indigenous weather knowledge, 10–11, **10–11**
instruments, 42–43, **42–43**
isobars, **44–45**, 45

K

Kakadu, 8, **8**
kangaroos, **9**
Kata Tjuta, 28
Kati Thanda see Lake Eyre/ Kati Thanda
knots, 28
kunanyi/Mount Wellington, 35

L

La Niña, 48
Lake Eyre/Kati Thanda, 35, **35**, 51
Lake Margaret, 34
lakes, 18, 34, 35, **35**, 50, 51
Latin, 16, 17
levees, 37
life jackets, **36**
lightning, 11, **11**, 17, **17**, 26–27, **26–27**, 32, 37
Lightning Man, 11, 58, **58**
lightning rods, 37, **37**
lizards, **13**, 34
low pressure system, 28, 29, 45, **45**

M

Mackellar, Dorothea, 58
mackerel sky, 17

Index

Madigan, Cecil, 57
magma, 53
magnetic poles, 9, **9**, 24
magnifying glasses, **21**, **51**, **54**
mantle, 53
maps, **8–9**, **13**, **32**, **33**, **34–35**, 44–45, **44–45**, 56, **56**, 59
Marble Bar, 34
mares' tails, 17
marsupial mouse see antechinus
Melbourne, 16, 35
mercury, 12, 42
mesosphere, 9
meteorologists, 43, 44, 45, 56, 57, **57**
meteors, 9
methane, 49
Millennium Drought, 32, **32**
millibars, 45
mist, 17
molluscs, 51, **51**
monoliths, 28, **28**, **34**
monsoons, 8
moon, 24, **24**
moonbows, 24, **24**
moths, 24, **24**
Mount Wellington see kunanyi/Mount Wellington
mountains, 12, 19, **20–21**, 35, 52, **52**
Murrumbidgee River, 11
music, 58

N

Namarrgon, 11
National Library of Australia, 56–59, **56–59**
neon, 8
New South Wales, 11, 32, **35**, 52, 53, 56
New Zealand, 28
Newcastle, 35
nitrogen, 8
North Pole, 9, **9**
Northern Hemisphere, 29
Northern Territory, 28, **34–35**, 53

O

ocean temperatures, 43, 48, 51, 52
oceans, 18, 29, 48, 50, 51, 52
Oodnadatta, 34
oral histories, 56, 58
oxygen, 8, 50
ozone layer, 9, **9**, 49, **49**

P

Pacific Ocean, 29
palm trees, **13**, **28–29**
penguins, **51**
Perth, 29, 34
petrichor, 19
phenomena, 10, 20
photographs, 43, 56–59, 56, **56**, 57, **57**, 58, **58**, **59**
photosynthesis, 50
pine cones, 41, **41**
planes, 17, **17**, 28, 33
plants, 10, 16, 18, 31, 41, 44, **48**, **49**, 50, 51, 59
playground equipment, 34, 58
pluviographs, 43
pollen, 16, 51, **51**
pollution, 17, 25, 48, 49
possums, **52**
precipitation, 16–17, 18–19, **18–19**, 20–21, **20–21**, 51
prisms, 24, **24**
protective clothing see clothing
protests, 59, **59**
pyjamas, 36, **36**

Q

Queensland, 32, 33, **35**, 48, 53
Queenslanders, 37

R

radar, 42, **42**
radiation, 8, 44, **44**, 52
radio, 36, 44, **59**
radiosondes, 42, **42**
rain, 11, 16, 17, 18–19, **18–19**, 34, 35, 36, 40, 41, 43, 44, **48**, **50**, **56**, 58
rain dances, **10**, 44
rain gauges, 42, **43**
Rainbow Serpent see Goorialla
rainbows, 24, **24**
raincoats, **36**
raindrops, 17, 18, **18**, 19, 24
rainmakers, 10, **10**
renewable energy, 52–53, **52–53**
robins, **20**
robots, 43
Russell, Henry, 56

S

sand, 28, **28**
sandbags, 37
sandcastles, **28**
sandstorms, 28, 40
satellites, 43, **43**
sea breezes, 29
sea levels, 48, 59
seabirds, 31, 41, **41**
seagulls, 41, **41**
seasonal calendars, 10–11, **10–11**
seasons, 8, 8, 10–11, **10–11**
seaweed, 41, **41**
sediment, 50, 51
serein, 19
sharks, 40, **40**
sheep, 13, 41, **41**
shells, 51, **51**
shockwaves, 26
signal flags see flags
silver iodide, 17
skeletons, **13**, 17, **17**, 51
skies, 24–25, **24–25**
sleet, 18, 20, 21
smells, 11, 19
smog, 17

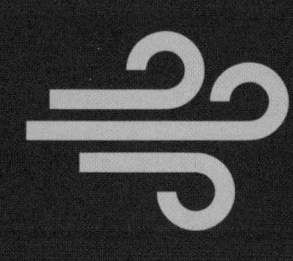

smoke, 17, 25, 29, 32, 45
snakes, **11**
snow, 12, 18, 19, 20–21, **20–21**, 34, 37, **37**
snow blindness, 20
snowballs, **21**
snowfields, 20
snowflakes, 21, **21**, 37
snowmen, 21, **21**
snowstorms, 42, 58, **58**
Snowy Mountains Scheme, 52, **52**
socks, 27, **27**
solar farms, 52
solar panels, 43, 52, **52**
solar power, 43, 52
songs, **58**
South Australia, 13, 29, 32, **34–35**, 51, 52
South Pole, **9**
Southerly Buster, 29
Southern Hemisphere, 24, 29, 33, 45
Southern Oscillation Index, 48
spectrum *see* colour spectrum
spring, 8, **10**, 50
state emergency services (SES), 36, 57
squalls, 28
Stevenson screen, 12, **12**
storm surges, 19, 33, **33**
storms, 8, 10, 17, 26, 27, 31, 32, 35, 36, 37, 40, 41, 42, 45, 51, 56, 57, **58**, 59
stormwater drains, 37
stratosphere, 9
Stretton, Alan, 58
subtropical climate zone, 8–9, **8–9**
sugarcane, 53, **53**
summer, 8, **10–11**, **12–13**, 29, 34, 50
sun, 8, 9, 16, 18, 24, **24**, 25, **25**, 28, 49, **49**, 52, **52**
sunburn, 20, 44
sunlight, 20, 24, 25, 50, 52
sunrise, 25, **25**
sunset, 25, **25**
sunshine, **34**, **35**
sunshowers, 19
supercells, 33
supercomputers, 43
superstorms, 29
Sydney, 21, 29, 33, **35**, **46**, 49

Sydney Observatory, 56

T
Tasmania, **35**, 52, 53
television, 44, **45**
temperate climate zone, 8–9, **8–9**
temperature, 12, **12**, 13, 20, 21, 29, 34, 35, 42, **42**, 43, 44, **44**, 48, 48–49, 50, 51, **52**, 52, **57**, 59
tempests *see* storms
thermal power, 53
thermometers, 12, **12**, 42, **42**, 44, **44**, 48, 57
thermosphere, 9
thunder, 11, 17, 26, **26**, 27, 32
thunderclouds, 17, **17**, 21
thunderstorms, 19, 26–27, 33
tide gauges, **56**
Top End, 8
tornadoes, 28, 32
transducers, **42**
tree rings, 50, **50–51**
trees, **11**, 12, 13, **13**, 27, **27**, 28, **28–29**, 32, 37, 41, 49, 50, **50**
tropical climate zone, 8–9, **8–9**, 13
troposphere, 9
tsunamis, 59
Tully, 35
turtles, 48, **48**
twisters *see* tornadoes
typhoons, 28

U
ultraviolet radiation, 44, **44**, 49
Uluru, 28, **28**, 34, **34**
umbrellas, **12–13**, 18, 27, **35**, 36, **58–59**
UV Index, 44, **44**

V
Victoria, 10, 32, 34, **35**
virga, 19
volcanoes, 25, 51

W
warm fronts, 45, **45**
water, 18–19, **18–19**
water cycle, **18**
water droplets, **16**, 18, 24, 25
water vapour, **16**, 17, 18, 25, **50**
waterholes, 41
waterspouts, 19, 28
wattle trees *see* gidgee
wave power, 53
wavelengths, 25, **25**
weather icons *see* icons
weather maps, 44–45, **44–45**
weather presenters, 44
weather stations, 12, **12**, 42, **42**, 43, 56
weathercocks, 43
weatherproofing, 36–37, **36–37**
Western Australia, 13, 29, **34**, 53
wet season, 8, 11, 13
whirlwinds, 28
White Cliffs, 52
whiteouts, 21
wildflowers, **10**
willy-willies, 28
wind, 9, 28–29, **28–29**, 34, 35, 37, 42, 43, 52, 57
wind chill, 12, 21, 29
wind farms, 53
wind force, 29, **29**
wind speed, 29, 35, 43, **43**
wind turbines, 53, **53**
windsocks, 43, **43**
windvanes, 43
winter, 8, **11**, 20–21, **20–21**
Wiradjuri people, 11
Wragge, Clement, 56

X
X-rays, 51

Z
zippers, **26**

NLA publishing — The publishing imprint of the National Library of Australia

Title: Australia's Wild, Weird, Wonderful Weather
Author: Stephanie Owen Reeder
Illustrator: Tania McCartney
ISBN: 9780642279637
Published by NLA Publishing
Canberra ACT 2600

© National Library of Australia 2020

Text © Stephanie Owen Reeder
Illustrations © Tania McCartney

Books published by the National Library of Australia further the Library's objectives to produce publications that interpret the Library's collection and contribute to the vitality of Australian culture and history.

Every reasonable endeavour has been made to contact the copyright holders. Where this has not been possible, the copyright holders are invited to contact the publisher.

First Nations peoples are advised this book contains content that may be considered culturally sensitive.

The views expressed in this book are those of the author and do not necessarily reflect the views of the National Library of Australia.

This book is copyright in all countries subscribing to the Berne Convention. Apart from any fair dealing for the purpose of research and study, criticism or review, as permitted under the *Copyright Act 1968*, no part may be reproduced by any process without written permission. Enquiries should be made to the publisher.

Commissioning Publisher: Susan Hall
Editor: Katherine Crane
Graphic designer: Tania McCartney
Cover: Tania McCartney
Indexer: Stephanie Owen Reeder
Image coordinator: Jemma Posch
Production coordinators: Rachael Warren and Dian Gargano
Printed in China by Asia Pacific Offset

The illustrations in this book were created digitally, utilising hand-printed and digital textures, as well as some hand-painted imagery.

Find out more about NLA Publishing at publishing.nla.gov.au.

For teachers' notes, go to publishing.nla.gov.au/pages/teachers-notes.do.

ACKNOWLEDGEMENTS

Creating this book would not have been possible without the talented team at NLA Publishing, including our brilliant and incredibly supportive publisher Susan Hall, editor Katherine Crane and our Indigenous Australian content and weather consultants. And, of course, we couldn't have produced this book without the ongoing support of our families, who now know way more about the weather than they ever imagined they would! Working together on this project has been a wonderful adventure. It has made us realise what an amazing country we live in, but also what a fragile and vulnerable planet we inhabit.

STEPHANIE OWEN REEDER was the 2019 recipient of the CBCA Laurie Copping Award for Distinguished Service to Children's Literature. Her recent books include *Trouble in the Surf*, *Story Time Stars* and *Will the Wonderkid*. She is also the author of the award-winning Heritage Heroes series, which includes *Amazing Grace* (NSW Premier's History Award 2012) and *Lennie the Legend* (CBCA Book of the Year Award 2016).

TANIA McCARTNEY is an award-winning author/illustrator of over 50 books, including *Mamie*, *Fauna: Australia's Most Curious Creatures*, *I Heart the World*, and junior fiction series *Evie and Pog*. The Founder of Kids' Book Review and the Happy Book Podcast, her awards include the SCBWI Crystal Kite Award (for Australia/New Zealand) and the CBCA Laurie Copping Award for Distinguished Service to Children's Literature.

A catalogue record for this book is available from the National Library of Australia